Welcome

111

FAVOURITES

31

61

WELCOME TO OUR THIRD ANNUAL RECIPE YEARBOOK. It's been an eventful and exciting year, and we've been lucky enough to have some wonderful contributors share their recipes and stories with us. I think this year's book reflects the quality and diversity of the mag and I'm excited to be getting this out for all of you to enjoy.

On average, each issue of our magazine contains over 100 recipes; that's almost a whole cookbook's worth! So, as you can probably imagine, choosing our favourites from the masses of lovely things we've cooked, commissioned (and consumed!) is hard work. We've concentrated on food that gets us all excited. The sort of dishes we want to come home to, or feed our friends on those special occasions. I hope you find plenty in here to keep you and your nearest and dearest happy. Here's to you, and another year of delicious food.

Editor at Large

In our third Recipe Yearbook you will find an inspiring collection of our favourite recipes from the past year of *Jamie Magazine*. If this is the first time you've seen a *Jamie* publication, the yearbook is a great introduction to our exciting world. As always, the recipes have been carefully tested in the *Jamie* kitchens, so you can be sure they work. This year, we've also added a guide to help you plan meals around seasonal produce. Our thanks go to Jamie and everyone else who helps create the recipes, and to the photographers who bring them to life on our pages. I don't want to play favourites, but I have to admit the Barbecoa burger (page 111), rhubarb and custard fairy cakes (page 126), French onion soup (page 31) and anchoïade bouzigode (page 61) have all been seen quite a bit in my kitchen this year. Enjoy your cooking, and eating!

andyharris

Editor

9

91

149

71

27

107

ALL RECIPES TESTED IN THE JAMIE OLIVER KITCHENS

37

125

53

Contents

Food for all seasons

Food tastes better when it's in season. Eat well year round with our produce guide

Summer

BASIL There are many different species of this aromatic, much-loved herb, from the large-leafed common or sweet basil to the fragrant , aniseedy Thai variety. *Summer roast chicken, page 101*

AUBERGINES Don't worry about salting these glossy beauties – today's available varieties tend not to be as bitter as earlier types, so they don't need it. *Melanzane parmigiana, page 64*

COURGETTES Gardeners: if you end up with a glut of these, don't let them go to waste – make a chutney and it'll be lovely by the time Christmas comes around. *Courgette carbonara, page 44*

TOMATOES Originally from Peru, tomatoes were once thought poisonous and were only ornamental. *BBQ sardines with gazpacho shots, page 80*

WATERMELON This thirst-quenching giant is great in salads, sorbets and classy cocktails (try combining its juice with gin, vodka or watermelon liqueur). *Asian-style watermelon salad, page 54*

ELDERFLOWERS A cordial made from these fleeting, delicate blooms can be used as a fragrant base for summery sorbets, sparkling wine and gorgeous cakes **Pistachio, yoghurt and elderflower cake, page 142**

Spring

BROAD BEANS A good source of vitamin C and protein, the broad bean is a great friend of all things pig-related. When they're young and tender, try them with their pods on. *Broad bean, ham & mint soup, page 28*

PEAS Try to cook fresh peas as soon after they're picked as you can – they'll become tougher and drier the longer you leave them, and will take a bit longer to cook. *Pea, mint & basil arancini cakes, page 49*

TROUT Oily fish such as trout and salmon are great sources of omega-3 fatty acids, which are important for brain function. **Barbecued trout in newspaper, page 76**

LEEKS Milder and sweeter than their onion relatives, leeks are at their best from November right through to April and are a fantastic flavour base for lots of dishes. *Leeks with mustard & dill vinaigrette & feta, page 58*

SORREL This slightly bitter-tasting plant (its name comes from the old French word for sour) is a tangy, traditional partner to fish dishes. It's also delicious in salads when the leaves are really young – use it like baby spinach. *Brill with sorrel sauce, page 88*

RHUBARB Outdoor-grown rhubarb appears in April; the more delicate 'forced' rhubarb is sold between January and March. Both have a sourness that suits rich or creamy dishes. *Vegan chocolate tart with rhubarb, page 136*

Autumn

APPLES The British climate is great for apples – we've got more than 2,000 cultivated varieties in the UK. This versatile fruit is easy to grow and great to cook with, and graces everything from savoury stews to delectable desserts. *Croustade, page 134*

SQUASH These come in all shapes and sizes. Butternut is great pals with a huge range of foods, from aromatic cinnamon to salty pancetta and feta. *Butternut squash & pancetta risotto, page 49*

FIGS Grown across the Med, fresh figs are exported from late summer to autumn. They're lovely with goat's cheese and prosciutto, and desserts. **Fig & olive oil cake, page 126**

PEARS The Romans were big fans – as well as eating pears, they made them into booze. Today you can raise a glass of perry, but we prefer them in salads, chutneys, with blue cheese, or baked in puddings or cakes. *Warm baked pear salad, page 54*

PLUMS There are hundreds of varieties of this sweet yet tart stone fruit, from red Victorias to lime-hued greengages. *Plum ripple ice cream, page 129*

RABBIT August through to February is the best time to get hold of wild rabbit, which is smaller and has a deeper, more gamey flavour than its farmed cousin. *Rabbit with potato & cider gratin, page 119*

Winter

KALE Available in curly and non-curly guises, this dark-green superfood is packed with iron, magnesium, calcium and vitamin C. **Caldo verde, page 35**

CAULIFLOWER Everyone is familiar with the big, white variety, but there have also been sightings of orange, bright green and even purple cauliflowers. *Whiting, leek & cauliflower gratin, page 83*

BEETROOT Step away from the pickled version – there's a wonderful world of lovely fresh beetroot out there! Check out the gorgeous pink and white Italian *chioggia* variety. *Mandolin salad, page 57*

GUINEA FOWL Greek legend says the grief-stricken sisters of murdered Prince Meleager (the birds are in the *meleagris* genus) turned into guinea fowl, and their tears became the birds' white markings. *Braised guinea fowls, root veg & lentils, page 104*

BLOOD ORANGES The spectacular crimson flesh of these intensely sweet fruits is owed to the presence of anthocyanin, the pigment found in red flowers. *Blood orange & fennel salad, page 64*

POMEGRANATES In the 18th century, the United States' third president, Thomas Jefferson, had a go at growing this wonder fruit at his Virginia farm. *Pomegranate & chicken stew, page 94*

Photography © David Loftus, James Lyndsay, Matt Rus

EVENT CATERING JUST GOT
STONKINGLY GOOD

A HOME IS BETTER THAN A HOUSE, A FRIEND IS BETTER THAN A STRANGER... A FEAST IS BETTER THAN A MEAL!

Jamie Oliver's Fabulous Feasts is taking the event catering world by storm... We're upping the ante, challenging the mundane and engaging customers with a truly unique offering. We believe in British and actively work closely with British growers and farmers wherever possible - but if taking a swim off our shores means getting the best ingredients, then that's what we'll do. We then add Jamie's creative twist and flair to dishes and deliver mind-blowing food, finished with a dollop of theatre and humour.

With a hugely experienced team, oozing passion, we're able to cater across a raft of different areas; from hospitality offerings and private parties, to public catering or a fixed offer from a venue.

Our vibrant menus focus on making your event memorable – to keep people talking long after the day's over. The proof's in the pudding (with thanks to our lovely customers!):

"We are in awe as to how you can provide such high quality food, with such lovely service…"

"Fabulous Feasts have really raised the bar in festival food to an unbelievable height! I had vertigo every time I ate lunch with them! Such a pleasure to work with…"

"Your team delivered high end restaurant quality in the middle of a field. Just fantastic!"

Get in touch today to find out more about how we can make your event go off with a real bang!

JAMIE OLIVER'S FABULOUS FEASTS
www.jamieoliver.com/fabulousfeasts

Charbridge Way • Bicester • Oxfordshire OX26 4SW • T. +44(0)1869 365795 • info@fabulousfeasts.co.uk

SNACKS AND STARTERS

EGGY CRUMPETS

HOMEMADE GRANOLA;
PLUM COMPOTE

EGGY CRUMPETS

This twist on french toast is also good served with crisp bacon. If you want to halve the proportions, use 2 small eggs and a pinch of cinnamon.

Serves 8

- 3 eggs
- 90ml milk
- ¾ tsp ground cinnamon
- 8 crumpets, halved
- A knob of butter
- Berries, crème fraîche or yoghurt and honey, to serve

1 Beat together the eggs, milk and cinnamon in a bowl. Place the crumpets in the mixture and allow them to soak a little. Melt the butter in a pan and fry the crumpets, in batches, for a couple of minutes each side until golden-brown. Keep the cooked ones warm in a low oven. Serve with berries, crème fraîche or yoghurt and a drizzle of honey.

HOMEMADE GRANOLA

Makes about 1.8kg

- 600g oats
- 450g mixed nuts
- 150g golden linseed
- 150g sunflower seeds
- 150g dried figs
- 150g dried apricots
- 9 tbsp honey
- 9 tbsp marmalade
- Yoghurt or milk and plum compote (below), to serve

1 Preheat the oven to 170C/gas 3 and line 2 oven trays with baking paper. Combine the oats, nuts, seeds, dried fruit, honey and marmalade in a bowl. Spread the mixture flat on the 2 trays and bake for 40-50 minutes, stirring halfway. Allow it to cool, then transfer to a clean, airtight jar. Serve the granola with yoghurt or milk and compote.

PLUM COMPOTE

Makes 380g

- 6 plums
- 35g sugar
- 1 vanilla pod, split in half lengthways

1 Place the plums in a saucepan with the sugar, vanilla and 200ml water. Slowly bring to the boil, allowing the sugar to dissolve, then simmer for 18-20 minutes, until the fruit breaks down. Transfer the compote to a sterilised jar while hot. Seal and store in the fridge for up to 1 week. Otherwise, leave to cool and enjoy on the same day.

POTATO & CHORIZO BREAKFAST HASH

Serves 2

- Olive oil
- 1 large onion, diced
- 1 garlic clove, chopped
- 120g chorizo, chopped
- 2-3 cooked potatoes, diced
- 2 eggs
- A small bunch of parsley, chopped

1 Preheat the oven to 180C/gas 4. Add a little olive oil to an ovenproof pan and fry the onion and garlic over a low heat until the onion is soft. Add the chorizo to the pan and fry for 2-3 minutes, until it begins to colour.
2 Add the cooked potatoes and fry for a further 5 minutes, then crack the eggs on top. Bake in the oven for 8 minutes, or until the egg whites are set but the yolks are still runny. Sprinkle with salt, pepper and chopped parsley to serve.

POTATO & CHORIZO BREAKFAST HASH

ASIAN FRIED EGGS WITH CHILLIES

Cracking eggs

Nothing sets you up for the day like an egg. If you have a soft spot for scrambled, try frying shredded courgette and basil, or sliced mushrooms and thyme in the pan before adding the eggs. If you're fond of a fried egg, sandwich one between some toasted sourdough or a muffin with chorizo, prosciutto or smoked salmon. For a bit of fun, place a toasted bagel cut-side up in a pan and crack an egg into the hole before grilling. Top with roasted tomato sauce or bacon and cover with the other bagel half. If you're partial to poached, sauté some sorrel or spinach, add a dash of crème fraîche and spoon over your usual eggs on toast. Biased towards baked eggs? Butter ramekins and line with bread before adding the eggs, then scoop out and serve in the bread shells. You can also layer the ramekins with artichoke hearts or smoked fish, and drizzle with cream before baking.

BAKED EGGS WITH SERRANO HAM

ASIAN FRIED EGGS WITH CHILLIES

Called 'son-in-law eggs' in Thailand, these spicy, crispy treats are well worth the effort of deep-frying.

Serves 4 as a starter

- 4 eggs
- Groundnut oil, for deep-frying
- 3 garlic cloves, thinly sliced
- 2 red chillies, thinly sliced
- 4 shallots, thinly sliced
- A handful of coriander cress or chopped coriander
- A handful of toasted peanuts

Dressing

- 2 tbsp fish sauce
- 3 tbsp grated palm sugar
- 3 tbsp tamarind purée

1 Place the eggs in a saucepan of cold water, bring to the boil and cook for 4 minutes, until they're just hard.

Drain, cool the eggs in cold water then peel and set aside in the same water.
2 Pour 10cm oil into a large pan and slowly heat. Meanwhile, put all the dressing ingredients in a small pan and gently cook, stirring, until the sugar dissolves. Set aside to cool.
3 The oil is hot enough when a piece of bread turns brown in about 3 minutes. Deep-fry the garlic, chillies and shallots until golden. Remove with a slotted spoon and drain on paper towel.
4 Pat the eggs dry with paper towel. Using a spoon, slide them into the oil one at a time. Deep-fry for 6–8 minutes, or until golden. Remove with a slotted spoon and drain on paper towel.
5 Slice the eggs in half and arrange on a plate. Spoon over the dressing, crispy garlic, chillies and shallots, then top with the coriander cress, or coriander, and peanuts. Serve immediately.

BAKED EGGS WITH SERRANO HAM

Serves 2

- Olive oil
- 4 serrano ham slices
- 4 eggs
- A chunk of manchego
- A few sage leaves
- Toast or crostini, to serve

1 Preheat the grill to high. Add a drizzle of olive oil to a small ovenproof pan and, once hot, fry the ham over a high heat until slightly crisp.
2 Create 4 spaces around the meat and crack the eggs into them. Season with sea salt and black pepper, and fry for 1 minute. Grate a little manchego over each egg, scatter with sage leaves and pop under the hot grill for 2–3 minutes, until cooked to your liking. Serve with the toast or crostini.

PANCAKE INGREDIENTS

BANANA PANCAKES

1 Cut 2 bananas into slices. Melt a little butter in a pan, then add the bananas and a squeeze of honey. Fry until golden brown, then keep warm. To serve, layer up the pancakes and bananas. Grate over the zest of 1 lime and serve with a drizzle of honey.

BERRY GOOD PANCAKES

1 Heat a nonstick frying pan and fry 6 rashers of streaky bacon until lovely and crisp. When the pancakes are half cooked, dot a handful of blueberries across them, let them set, then flip and finish cooking according to the recipe. Serve with the bacon, a drizzle of maple syrup, plus extra blueberries if you like.

DESSERT APPLE PANCAKES

1 Quarter and core 2 eating apples, then slice each quarter into 4. Melt a dot of butter in a frying pan and fry the apples until browned. Serve the pancakes with the apples, good-quality ice cream and a dash of cinnamon.

COCONUT PANCAKES WITH POMEGRANATE JEWELS

1 Cut a pomegranate in half – watch out, it can be messy! Get a mixing bowl and hold the fruit, seed-side down, above the bowl. Use a wooden spoon to tap the back of the pomegranate so the seeds fall into the bowl. Fill the bowl with water, then pick out any white bits that float to the top before gently draining away the water.
2 Mix about 8 tablespoons of desiccated coconut into your pancake batter, then fry as before. To serve, top the coconut pancakes with a spoonful or two of plain yoghurt and some of the pomegranate seeds, then finely grate over the zest of a lime and an orange.

ONE-CUP PANCAKES

This is a great recipe to make with the kids. You don't need any fancy equipment - a mug is fine for measuring the main ingredients.
Makes 6 pancakes (serves 3)
- 1 egg
- 1 cup self-raising flour
- 1 tsp baking powder (optional)
- 1 cup milk
- 20g butter

1 Crack the egg into a large bowl, then add the flour, baking powder, milk and a tiny pinch of sea salt. Whisk together until you have a smooth batter. Cover your bowl in clingfilm and put to one side to rest. Now get your toppings ready, using our ideas on the right.

2 Put a large frying pan over a medium heat and melt half the butter. Once it is starting to bubble, spoon in the pancake batter, so it is roughly the size of an orange - you should be able to fit 2-3 pancakes in the pan.
3 Cook the pancakes for 1-2 minutes, until little bubbles rise up to the top. Use a fish slice or heatproof spatula to turn them over. Cook for another minute or so, till golden on both sides.
4 When they are done, transfer the pancakes to a plate and cover with foil to keep warm. Carefully wipe the pan clean with kitchen paper, then add the remaining butter and keep going until all the batter is used up. Serve the pancakes with our toppings, or add a little sugar and a squeeze of lemon.

BERRY GOOD PANCAKES

COCONUT PANCAKES WITH POMEGRANATE JEWELS

DESSERT APPLE PANCAKES

BANANA PANCAKES

FIGS WITH PINE NUTS & GOAT'S CURD

SOUFFLE AU FROMAGE

ONION TARTE TATIN

Serves 4-6

- 750g mixed onions and shallots
- A knob of butter
- Olive oil
- A few thyme sprigs
- ½ tbsp sugar
- 1 tbsp balsamic vinegar
- 250g readymade butter puff pastry
- Goat's cheese chunks or grated parmesan, to serve

1 Preheat the oven to 200C/gas 6. Cut the small onions in half and large ones into wedges. In a round 23cm ovenproof pan, melt the butter with a glug of oil, add the thyme and onions, sprinkle over the sugar, drizzle with the balsamic vinegar and season well. Cook over a low heat for 15 minutes, stirring occasionally, until caramelised.
2 When the onions are almost ready, roll out the pastry on a floured board and cut a circle just larger than the pan. Remove the pan from the heat and gently drape your pastry over it, tucking the ends into the base, then bake for 20-25 minutes, or until golden. Leave the tart to rest for 5 minutes before carefully turning out onto a platter or board. Top with the chunks of goat's cheese or grated parmesan.

FIGS WITH PINE NUTS & GOAT'S CURD

Serves 4-6

- 2 tbsp honey
- A few thyme sprigs
- 6 figs, halved
- 125g soft goat's curd or cheese
- 2 tbsp pine nuts, toasted

1 Gently warm the honey and thyme in a small saucepan over a medium heat for a few minutes, then leave to infuse.
2 Heat a griddle pan over a high heat. Place the figs on the griddle, cut-side down, and cook until charred. Season well. Top each fig half with a spoonful of goat's curd, then drizzle with the thyme honey and scatter over the pine nuts.

SOUFFLE AU FROMAGE
Cheese soufflé

Soufflés strike fear into the hearts of even the bravest cooks, but when there's only you to impress, why not give one a try?

Serves 1

- 6-8 cherry tomatoes, on the vine
- Olive oil
- Balsamic vinegar
- 1 tsp butter, plus extra for greasing
- 1 heaped tsp flour, plus extra for dusting
- 75ml whole milk
- 35g emmental or gruyère, grated
- A small pinch of ground nutmeg
- 1 egg, separated

1 Preheat the oven to 200C/gas 6. Place the tomatoes in a small roasting pan, drizzle with olive oil and balsamic vinegar, season, then set aside.
2 Thoroughly grease a 200ml ramekin with butter. Dust with a little flour and shake off the excess. Make a béchamel sauce: melt the butter in a small pan, add the flour and stir until you have a smooth paste. Gradually stir in the milk, bring to a simmer and cook over a medium heat, stirring constantly, for 2-3 minutes, till the sauce thickens. Stir in the cheese and nutmeg, season, then leave to cool for a few minutes.
3 Whisk the egg white to soft peaks. Add the egg yolk to the béchamel and mix to combine. Stir a spoonful of the white into the mixture, then gently fold in the remaining white. Pour the mixture into the ramekin and run your finger around the rim to help the soufflé rise straight. Place on a baking tray and bake with the tomatoes for 15-20 minutes, until risen and golden.

INDIAN DOSA

MEAT BRIKS

INDIAN DOSA
Serves 6-8
- 2 baking potatoes
- 2 sweet potatoes
- Olive oil
- 1 dried red chilli, finely sliced
- 1 fresh red chilli, finely sliced
- 1cm piece of ginger, finely sliced
- 1½ tsp mustard seeds
- 1 tsp turmeric
- Juice of ½ lime, plus wedges to serve
- 4 spring onions, finely sliced
- A few coriander sprigs, chopped
- Mint yoghurt, chutney, lime, to serve

Dosa batter
- 1 cup gram (chickpea) flour
- 1 cup flour
- ½ tsp bicarbonate of soda
- 2½ tsp mustard seeds

1 Preheat the oven to 200C/gas 6. Bake all the potatoes for 1 hour or until soft. Cut open and scoop the flesh into a bowl. Roughly mash then set aside.
2 Heat a glug of oil over a medium heat in a pan. Add the chillies, ginger and spices, season, then cook until the seeds start popping. Mix with potatoes. Season again, stir in the lime juice, spring onions and coriander, then set aside.
3 Slowly whisk in about 400ml water to the dosa batter ingredients with a pinch of salt, to give a loose batter. Add a splash of oil to a pan over a medium-high heat and wipe out with kitchen paper. Add a spoonful of batter and twist the pan so it coats the base and slips up the edges. When lots of bubbles appear, spread a few heaped teaspoons of potato filling across the dosa. Once the base is crispy, loosely roll up the dosa in the pan. Serve with yoghurt, chutney and lime wedges.

MEAT BRIKS
Serves 4
- Olive oil
- 350g minced lamb
- 1 onion, grated
- 2 garlic cloves, chopped
- 1 tsp each paprika, ground cinnamon, cumin and ginger
- 8 filo sheets
- Harissa sauce, to serve

1 Add a splash of oil to a large pan and fry the lamb until brown and cooked, about 5-8 minutes. Set aside.
2 In the same pan, sauté the onion and garlic for 3-4 minutes in a little more oil. Add the spices and stir for 2-3 minutes. Return the lamb to the pan and cook for 10 minutes, then leave to cool.
3 Divide the meat between the filo sheets, then roll into cigar shapes.
4 Heat a splash of oil in a large pan. Fry 2-3 cigars at a time for 3-5 minutes until golden. Serve with harissa sauce.

PORK DUMPLINGS
Makes 24
- 150g flour, plus extra
- 2 tbsp vegetable oil

Filling
- 120g savoy cabbage, shredded
- 200g pork mince
- 3 spring onions, chopped
- 1 tbsp rice wine vinegar
- 1 tsp soy sauce
- 1 tsp sesame oil

Dipping sauce
- 4 tbsp soy sauce
- 1 tsp sesame oil
- Chopped chilli, to taste

1 Slowly mix 90ml cold water into the flour for a firm dough. Roll into a tube, wrap in clingfilm, chill for 20-30 minutes.
2 On a floured surface, cut the dough into 24 pieces and roll into 10cm circles. Mix the filling ingredients together and place 1 heaped teaspoon in the centre of each dough circle. Brush edges with water, bring together, press to seal.
3 Heat half the veg oil in a nonstick pan over a medium-high heat. Cook half the dumplings for 1-2 minutes, or till golden underneath. Add 200ml water, cover with foil, reduce heat and steam for 4-5 minutes, or till cooked. Keep warm.
4 Wipe out the pan, cook the rest of the dumplings. Combine sauce ingredients and serve with the dumplings.

PORK DUMPLINGS

MIXED HERB & GOAT'S CHEESE QUICHE

Serves 6-8

- A large handful of mixed herbs, such as tarragon, chives or mint, chopped
- 80g goat's cheese, crumbled
- 200ml crème fraîche
- 200ml milk
- 2 eggs, lightly beaten
- 2 egg yolks, lightly beaten
- A handful of micro herbs (optional) and baby salad leaves, to serve

Shortcrust pastry

- 250g flour
- 1 tsp salt
- 115g unsalted butter, diced
- 1 egg yolk

1 For the pastry, combine the flour and salt in a food processor. Add the butter and egg yolk and process for 1 minute. Add about 4 tablespoons of cold water and pulse until the dough is combined. Transfer to a lightly floured surface and gently knead with the heel of your hand for 2 minutes. Flatten into a disc, wrap in clingfilm and chill for at least 1 hour.
2 On a floured surface, roll the dough out to 5mm thick. Lay the pastry over a round 24cm tart tin, 3cm deep, and carefully press into the base and sides. Trim any excess. Line with 4 layers of clingfilm and chill for 30 minutes.
3 Preheat the oven to 180C/gas 4 and blind bake the pastry (see page 170). Cool in tin. Turn the oven to 190C/gas 5.
4 Place the tart case on an oven tray. Scatter over the herbs, then dot with the goat's cheese. Whisk together the crème fraîche, milk, eggs and egg yolks and seasoning. Pour into the case.
5 Bake the quiche for 30-35 minutes, or until the filling has set and the top is beginning to turn golden. Cool on the tray a little, then sprinkle with micro herbs and salad leaves before serving.

TOMATO, OLIVE, FETA & ANCHOVY TART

Serves 4-6

- Olive oil
- 1 red onion, finely sliced
- 2 garlic cloves, finely chopped
- 400g plum tomatoes, peeled, deseeded and chopped

TOMATO, OLIVE, FETA & ANCHOVY TART

- 1 tbsp tomato purée
- 6 thyme sprigs, leaves picked
- 100g feta, crumbled
- 75g kalamata olives
- 12 tinned anchovy fillets, drained

Crisp pastry

- 330g flour
- ½ tsp sugar
- 1 tsp salt
- 170g unsalted butter, diced

1 For the pastry, blitz the flour, sugar and salt in a food processor until combined. Add half the butter and process for 30 seconds, then add the remaining butter and process for 1 minute. Add 100ml cold water and pulse until large lumps form.
2 Transfer to a lightly floured surface and bring together into a rough dough. Knead the dough with the heel of your hand for 30 seconds, or until just combined. Flatten to a disc, wrap in clingfilm and chill for at least 1 hour.

3 Roll the pastry out to 5mm thick. Lay over a 35cm x 10cm tart tin and carefully press into the base and sides. Trim the excess. Line the case with 4 layers of clingfilm and chill for 30 minutes.
4 Preheat the oven to 180C/gas 4 and blind bake the pastry (see page 170), then set aside to cool in the tin.
5 Meanwhile, heat 1 tablespoon of olive oil in a large pan over a medium heat. Add the onion and garlic and cook for 4-5 minutes, or until softened. Add the tomatoes, tomato purée and thyme. Cook the mixture, stirring occasionally, for 20 minutes or until thickened. Remove from the heat and leave to cool.
6 Place the pastry case on an oven tray and spread the tomato mixture over the base. Scatter over the crumbled feta and olives, top with the anchovy fillets and drizzle with olive oil. Bake the tart in the oven for 30 minutes or until the top has caramelised slightly. Serve warm or cold with a green salad, if you like.

Make your own cinema snacks

Cinema snacks are typically expensive and predictable, so why not make your own? Popcorn couldn't be easier, but there are plenty of other ideas you can try. Load wooden skewers with a mixture of fruits and berries if you feel virtuous, or marshmallows and sweets if you're in a naughty mood. Stir roasted nuts into a mixture of melted honey, butter, brown sugar and cinnamon and dry out on baking paper for a sweet and crunchy snack. For something savoury, toss nuts and seeds in soy sauce and leave to colour slightly in a low oven. For a childhood classic, melt chocolate, butter and golden syrup and stir in cornflakes (and raisins, if you fancy). Scrunch together into small clusters and refrigerate overnight.

BASIC POPCORN

Make up a batch of popcorn, then add your choice of toppings from our suggestions - each one makes enough for this popcorn recipe.

Serves 4 as a snack

- 1-2 tbsp oil with a high smoking point, such as rapeseed, good-quality extra-virgin olive or sunflower
- 60g popping corn

1 Pour the oil into a large, heavy-based saucepan over a medium-high heat. Once hot, add the corn and shake the pan gently so the kernels are in 1 layer and coated in oil. Put the lid on and leave over the heat, shaking the pan every 30 seconds. The popcorn is ready when the pops are about 2-3 seconds apart. Tip into a large bowl and season with butter, sugar, salt, or one of the flavours we suggest here, while warm.

MARMITE

This popcorn tastes just like buttery Marmite on toast. If you usually spread your Marmite thickly, go for the full 2 teaspoons - or even more if you're a real Marmite fiend.

- 25g butter
- 1-2 tsp Marmite

1 Preheat the oven to 150C/gas 2. Cover a baking tray with greaseproof paper.
2 Melt the butter in a small pan over a low heat and stir in the Marmite until you have a smooth, glossy liquid. Pour the mixture over the cooked popcorn and stir well until every piece is coated.

3 Spread the popcorn over the lined baking tray and place in the oven for 3-4 minutes to crisp up a little. Like classic Marmite on toast, it makes a great snack at any time of day.

ANCHOVY & ROSEMARY

This may sound strange, but it works beautifully. Rich and salty anchovy is perfectly balanced by fragrant rosemary. Using olive oil makes for a lighter snack; using butter makes it more decadent.

- 2 tbsp olive oil or 25g butter
- 5 tinned anchovy fillets, drained and finely chopped
- 3 rosemary sprigs, leaves picked and finely chopped

1 Add the oil or melt the butter in a pan over a medium heat. Add the anchovies and squash them with the back of a wooden spoon until they dissolve.
2 Remove the pan from the heat, stir in the rosemary leaves, then pour the topping over the cooked popcorn. Stir well to coat every piece, then tip into a serving bowl. This is especially delicious with a strong martini, a glass of champagne or a chilled dry white wine.

BACON & MAPLE SYRUP

It's worth tracking down authentic maple syrup, even if it costs more, as the artificial varieties tend to lack that distinctive smoky maple flavour.

- 5 smoked streaky bacon or pancetta rashers
- 3 tbsp maple syrup

1 Preheat the oven to 150C/gas 2. Cover a baking tray with greaseproof paper.
2 Fry the bacon in a pan over a medium heat until crisp. Drain on kitchen paper. When cool enough to handle, crumble the bacon over the warm cooked popcorn and pour over the maple syrup. Stir until coated, adding a drizzle more syrup if necessary. Taste, and season with sea salt if you like. Spread the popcorn over the lined baking tray and bake for 3-4 minutes to crisp up a little. Tip into a serving bowl and enjoy warm.

MEXICAN

This has serious Latin heat. You could add a splash of tequila, if you dare...

- 2 tbsp olive oil or 25g butter
- A pinch of cayenne or hot chilli powder
- 1 tsp ground cumin
- 1 tsp dried oregano
- 1 tsp smoked paprika
- Juice of ½ lime and zest of 1 lime

1 Heat the oil or melt the butter in a pan over a low heat. Stir in all the spices and cook for 1 minute or so before taking off the heat. Stir in the lime juice then pour the mixture over the warm popcorn, followed by a few pinches of sea salt. Stir well until every piece is coated, then tip into a serving bowl. Sprinkle with the lime zest and a little extra cayenne if you like a bit of a kick.

MARMITE

ANCHOVY & ROSEMARY

MEXICAN

BACON & MAPLE SYRUP

SAUSAGE & FENNEL MUFFINS

SAUSAGE & FENNEL MUFFINS
Makes 12

- 200g (about 3) Italian-style sausages
- 1 garlic clove, crushed
- ½ tsp dried chilli flakes
- 1 tsp fennel seeds, crushed
- 350g flour
- 1½ tbsp baking powder
- ½ bunch of spring onions, finely sliced
- 2 eggs
- 150ml olive oil
- 275ml milk
- 135ml buttermilk
- 200g cheddar, grated
- A few sprigs of flat-leaf parsley, leaves picked and chopped

1 Preheat the oven to 180C/gas 4 and line a muffin tray with cases. Squeeze the sausages out of their skins and fry in a dry pan over a high heat with the garlic, chilli and crushed fennel seeds until crumbled and crispy. Leave to cool.
2 In a large bowl, mix the flour, baking powder, most of the spring onion and seasoning. In a jug, whisk together the eggs, olive oil, milk and buttermilk.
3 Add most of the sausage and most of the cheese to the flour mixture. Make a well and pour in the wet ingredients. Add the parsley. Gently fold together but don't overmix – a few lumps are OK. Pour into the muffin cases, top with the rest of the spring onion, cheese and sausage and bake for 15–20 minutes till golden.

HOT CROSS BUNS
Serves 12

- 50g sugar
- 7g sachet dried yeast
- 450g flour
- 2 tsp mixed spice
- 100g mixed dried fruit (such as currants, sour cherries and sultanas)
- 25g chopped mixed peel
- Grated zest of 1 orange
- 1 egg, beaten
- 50g butter, melted, plus extra for greasing
- 50ml milk, warmed
- 1 egg, beaten

Decoration
- 100g flour mixed with about 50ml water to make a dough, or 100g readymade shortcrust pastry

HOT CROSS BUNS

Sticky glaze
- 2 tbsp sugar
- Juice of 1 orange

1 In a jug, mix 1 tsp of the sugar with the yeast and 150ml tepid water until frothy.
2 Sift the flour, 1 tsp salt and the mixed spice into a large bowl, then add the dried fruit, peel, orange zest and remaining sugar. Make a well in the middle and pour in the yeast mixture, then add the beaten egg, melted butter and 40ml of the milk. Using a fork or wooden spoon, stir in a circular motion until you have a dough. Add a little more milk if the mixture is too dry.
3 Knead on a floured surface until smooth and glossy, about 5 minutes. Place in a large mixing bowl and cover with a clean, damp tea towel. Leave in a warm place to prove until doubled in size, about 1 hour. Knock back and knead again to its original size, then divide into 12 evenly sized pieces.

4 Shape the dough into round buns and place on a lightly greased baking tray, spaced well apart. Cover with a damp tea towel and leave to rise again until doubled in size, about 35–40 minutes.
5 Meanwhile, preheat the oven to 220C/gas 7. For the decoration, place the dough or pastry on a floured surface and roll into a sausage about 1cm thick. Cut in half, and cut each half into 6. Roll out each piece again to make 2 thinner strips of about 5mm wide by 8cm long. You should have 24.
6 Brush the risen, uncooked buns with the beaten egg and lay the dough strips on top in the shape of a cross. Brush the crosses with the beaten egg and bake for 15 minutes, or until golden.
7 Meanwhile for the glaze, place the sugar and orange juice in a small pan and gently heat until the sugar is dissolved and the syrup is bubbling. Brush the buns with the glaze and eat immediately, or cool and serve toasted.

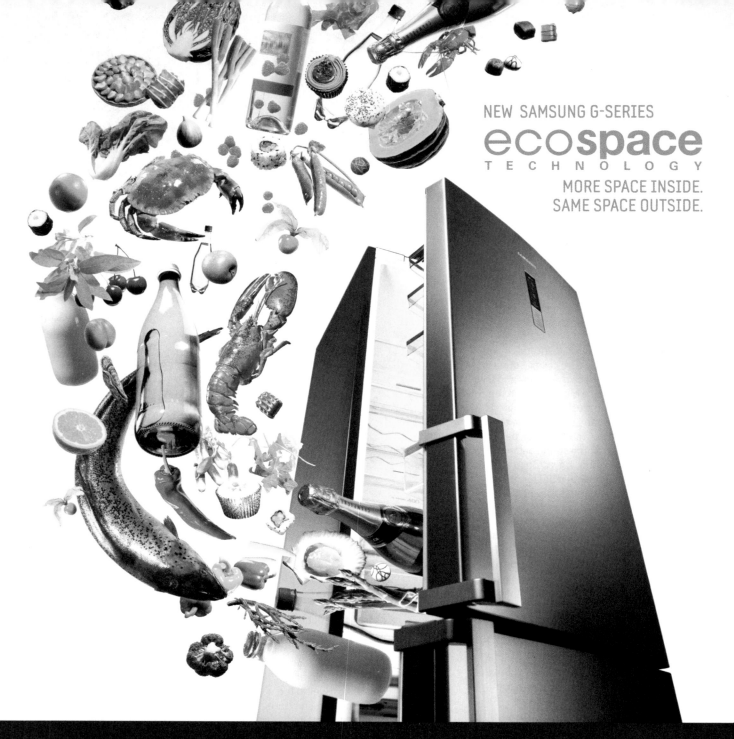

NEW SAMSUNG G-SERIES

ecospace
T E C H N O L O G Y

MORE SPACE INSIDE.
SAME SPACE OUTSIDE.

ENJOY MORE SPACE FOR THE FOOD YOU LOVE

Samsung presents its G-Series refrigeration range. Thanks to space
innovations, you can maximise your storage space and organise your
food more easily. Available in a variety of different sizes and colour
finishes, the G-Series is the perfect match for your kitchen.

Discover the range of Samsung Home Appliances at www.samsung.com/uk

Three Door   Side-by-Side   No Frost Combi

SOUPS

CHILLED AVOCADO & CUCUMBER SOUP

1 Split the bean pods and remove the beans. For this recipe, you don't have to double pod them, unless you want to, or they're mature. Set aside in a bowl.
2 Heat the olive oil in a large saucepan over a medium heat, then cook the onion, carrot and leek for 5-8 minutes, stirring occasionally, until softened. Add the garlic with the bay leaves, stir, and cook for a couple of minutes. Add the gammon and cook for 10 minutes more, stirring occasionally so everything cooks nice and evenly.
3 Pour in the stock and bring the soup up to the boil, then reduce the heat slightly and let everything bubble away gently for about 15 minutes, stirring occasionally, until the gammon is tender and cooked through.
4 Stir the mint leaves into the soup, with the broad beans. Cook everything for few more minutes, until the beans are just tender. Ladle into bowls, add a grind of black pepper, if you like, and serve with slices of crusty bread.

CHILLED AVOCADO & CUCUMBER SOUP

Creamy avocado and cooling cucumber make this perfect for a summer's day.

Serves 4

- 2 avocados, stoned, peeled and chopped
- 2 cucumbers, chopped
- 1-2 red chillies, chopped
- Juice of 2 lemons
- 200ml single cream
- 4 bacon rashers
- 2 tomatoes, finely chopped
- ½ red onion, finely chopped
- Extra-virgin olive oil

1 Place the avocado, cucumber, chilli, lemon juice and cream in a food processor or blender and blitz until smooth. Season and strain through a sieve into a bowl, then chill.
2 Fry the bacon until crisp. Finely chop. Garnish the soup with bacon, tomato and onion, and drizzle with oil to serve.

BROAD BEAN, HAM & MINT SOUP

This is a good recipe to make with children. They can pod the beans for you, measure the oil into the pan, crush the garlic and pick the mint leaves. Older kids can peel and chop the veg, as long as they're supervised. After all their hard work, they'll enjoy helping you to eat this hearty soup!

Serves 4

- 500g unpodded broad beans
- 2 tbsp olive oil
- 1 onion, diced
- 1 carrot, diced
- 1 leek, sliced
- 2 garlic cloves, crushed
- 2 bay leaves
- 300g unsmoked gammon, chopped or shredded
- 1 litre chicken or vegetable stock
- ½ bunch of mint, leaves picked, larger leaves torn
- Crusty bread, to serve

BORSCHT

Not pictured

Enjoy this colourful soup warm in the winter and cold in the summer.

Serves 4

- 500g beetroot, peeled
- About 4 tbsp sugar
- Juice of about ½ lemon
- 1 tbsp white wine vinegar
- Sour cream, to serve
- Chopped boiled egg, dill, white onion and cucumber, to serve (optional)

1 Cook the beetroot in boiling water until tender. Drain it, reserving the cooking water, then coarsely grate.
2 Pour 500ml of the hot cooking water into a large pan, season well and stir in the beetroot, sugar, lemon juice and vinegar. Taste, adding more sugar or lemon juice until the sweetness and acidity are to your liking. Heat the soup if you'd like to eat it warm, or allow it to cool, then refrigerate to eat chilled. Serve with a dollop of sour cream and any of the other garnishes you like.

BROAD BEAN, HAM & MINT SOUP

CLASSIC
DISH

CHICKPEA, ROSEMARY & PANCETTA SOUP

TOMATO & CHICKPEA SOUP

FRENCH ONION SOUP

Serves 4-6
- 80g butter
- 6 large onions, thinly sliced
- 1 tbsp thyme leaves
- 2 bay leaves
- 1 tbsp flour
- 200ml white wine
- 1.5 litres beef stock
- 12 slices of day-old baguette
- 150g grated gruyère

1 Melt the butter in a large pan. Stir in the onion, thyme and bay leaves, and season. Cook over a low heat for 40 minutes or until the onions are translucent and very soft, not coloured.
2 Sprinkle over the flour and mix well, then slowly add the wine, followed by the beef stock. Increase the heat and bring the soup to the boil, then simmer for 20 minutes. Remove the bay leaves and discard. Adjust the seasoning.
3 Arrange the bread on a baking tray, sprinkle over two-thirds of the gruyère and place under a hot grill for 2-3 minutes, until the cheese melts. Ladle the soup into warm bowls and top each one with a slice of cheesy bread. Scatter over the remaining gruyère, transfer the bowls to the baking tray and place under the hot grill for 2 minutes, until the cheese bubbles and turns golden. Serve immediately.

CHICKPEA, ROSEMARY & PANCETTA SOUP

Serves 4
- 2 onions, diced
- 2 garlic cloves, chopped
- 2 celery stalks, diced
- 8 slices of pancetta, 4 finely chopped, 4 whole
- 2 tbsp olive oil
- 3 rosemary sprigs
- 2 x 400g tins of chickpeas, drained
- 1 litre chicken or vegetable stock
- Juice of ¼–½ lemon
- Croutons and extra-virgin olive oil, to serve

1 Gently fry the onion, garlic, celery and chopped pancetta in the olive oil with the rosemary till the onion is soft. Add the chickpeas and cook for 5 minutes.
2 Pour in the stock, bring to the boil, then reduce the heat and simmer for 15 minutes. Season, then remove the rosemary. Add the lemon juice then transfer the soup to a food processor and blitz until puréed.
3 Fry the remaining pancetta till crisp. Sprinkle the croutons over the soup, top with the pancetta slices and drizzle with extra-virgin olive oil to serve.

TOMATO & CHICKPEA SOUP

Serves 4
- 2 tbsp olive oil
- 2 carrots, cut into strips
- 2 celery stalks, chopped
- 2 garlic cloves, finely chopped
- 1 red onion, sliced
- 2 bay leaves
- 1–2 tsp chilli flakes
- 2 tsp dried oregano
- 1 x 400g tin of chickpeas, drained
- 1 x 400g tin of chopped tomatoes
- 750ml vegetable stock
- 100g baby or frozen spinach

1 Heat the olive oil in a large frying pan. Add the chopped carrot, celery, garlic and sliced onion and cook till softened, then add the bay leaves, chilli flakes and oregano, and season well. Add the chickpeas, tomatoes and vegetable stock and bring to the boil.
2 Reduce the heat and simmer for 18-20 minutes, then add the spinach and turn off the heat. Leave the soup for a few minutes, stirring occasionally, until the spinach has wilted (if using frozen spinach, simmer till it's hot), then serve immediately.

BROCCOLI & SWEET POTATO SOUP

TORTILLA SOUP

BROCCOLI & SWEET POTATO SOUP
Serves 4
- 1 tbsp olive oil
- 1 onion, diced
- 2 garlic cloves, crushed
- 2-3 sweet potatoes (about 550g), cut into 2cm chunks
- 750ml chicken or vegetable stock
- 200g broccoli
- 2 tsp harissa

1 Heat the oil in a large pan and gently cook the onion for 5-7 minutes, until softened. Add the garlic and cook for 2-3 minutes. Add the sweet potatoes and cook for a few more minutes, then add the stock. Bring to the boil, then simmer for 15 minutes, adding the broccoli for the last 5 minutes; cook for a little more or less if necessary, until the vegetables are tender.
2 Transfer the sweet potato mixture to a food processor with the broccoli and blitz until puréed. To serve, reheat the soup and stir in the harissa.

TORTILLA SOUP
Serves 4
- Olive oil
- 2 onions, chopped
- 2 garlic cloves, sliced
- 1-2 red chillies, sliced
- 4 tomatoes, chopped
- 1 litre chicken stock
- 2 corn tortillas, cut into strips
- 250g cooked chicken, shredded
- 2 avocados, flesh sliced
- ½ bunch of coriander, leaves picked
- 1 lime, cut into 4 wedges

1 Heat a little oil in a large pan and sauté the onion, garlic and chilli over a medium heat for 5 minutes, until soft but not coloured. Add the tomatoes and cook for 10 minutes. Season, pour in the stock, then simmer for 20 minutes.
2 Meanwhile, in a large frying pan, fry the tortilla strips in a little olive oil until golden. Transfer them to kitchen paper to drain, then sprinkle with salt.
3 Divide the chicken between 4 bowls and pour in the soup. Top with the tortilla strips, avocado and coriander leaves. Serve with lime wedges.

MEATBALL SOUP
Make meat stretch further with this easy store-cupboard soup. Just use whatever vegetables you have.
Serves 8
- Olive oil
- 1 large carrot, chopped
- ½ small celery, trimmed and chopped
- 1 large leek, chopped
- 1 small onion, chopped
- 2 bay leaves
- 6 thyme sprigs, leaves picked
- 2 x 400g tins of beans, such as cannellini or red kidney, drained
- 2 x 400g tins of tomatoes
- Crusty bread, to serve

Meatballs
- 200g minced lean beef
- 200g minced lean pork
- 1 small onion, finely grated
- 1 large garlic clove, finely grated
- 60g breadcrumbs
- ½ bunch of parsley, leaves picked and finely chopped

1 For the meatballs, put all ingredients in a bowl and season well. Using wet hands, scrunch till well combined (to check the seasoning, fry a small piece and taste), then roll the mixture into small balls about 2cm wide.
2 For the soup, put a small drizzle of oil in a large saucepan over a low-medium heat and cook the carrot, celery, leek and onion till soft but not coloured. Add the bay and thyme leaves with 1.2 litres water and bring to a simmer. Stir in the beans and tomatoes. Season.
3 When the soup is simmering, add the meatballs. As they're small, they won't take long to cook and will add flavour to the soup. When they're cooked through, ladle the soup into bowls. If you fancy, serve with some good bread.

MEATBALL SOUP

CALDO VERDE

CHICKEN NOODLE SOUP

EASY LEEK SOUP

Serves 4-6
- 4 large leeks, sautéed
- 1 litre beef stock
- 4-6 slices of ciabatta
- 1 garlic clove, halved
- 40g-60g gruyère, grated (optional)
- Extra-virgin olive oil

1 Place the leeks and stock in a large pan and bring to the boil then simmer for 15 minutes; season. Toast the bread under a hot grill, then rub with the cut side of the garlic. Top with the cheese, if using, and grill until melted. Drizzle oil over the soup and serve with the toasts.

CALDO VERDE

Roll up the kale leaves tightly (cut out the thick stems first), then cut into wafer-thin strips as in Portugal, where this soup is eaten on a daily basis.
Serves 4
- 5 tbsp extra-virgin olive oil
- 1 large onion, finely chopped
- 2 garlic cloves, chopped
- 700g potatoes, diced
- 300g kale or cavolo nero, finely shredded
- 150g chorizo, sliced
- Paprika, to taste
- Extra-virgin olive oil and cornbread (see note), to serve

1 Heat 4 tablespoons of the olive oil in a heavy saucepan over a medium heat and fry the onion and garlic for 5 minutes, or until they begin to soften. Stir in the potatoes, season with salt, and cook for 5 minutes. Add 1.25 litres water and simmer for 20 minutes or until the potatoes are soft. Mash the potatoes into a smooth purée. Add the kale and simmer for 5 minutes.
2 Meanwhile, heat the remaining oil in a frying pan over a medium heat and fry the chorizo, sprinkling paprika over it, for 3-4 minutes. Add the chorizo to the soup, then ladle into bowls and season with black pepper. Serve with a swirl of the olive oil and slices of cornbread.
Note You can buy great cornbread at Portuguese stores such as London's Lisboa Delicatessen (54 Golborne Road, W10; 020 8969 1052), or substitute it with some decent ciabatta.

CHICKEN NOODLE SOUP

Serves 6
- 1 medium chicken (about 1.4kg)
- 1 celery heart, roughly chopped
- 200g small carrots
- 2 garlic cloves, peeled but whole
- 100g baby leeks
- 200g small onions
- 2-3 bay leaves
- A handful of parsley stalks
- A thumb-sized knob of ginger, peeled but whole
- A large splash of dry sherry
- A pinch of saffron
- A splash of sweet ginger vinegar (optional, see note)
- 300g mixed flat pasta shapes

1 Place the chicken, celery, carrots, garlic, leeks, onions, bay, parsley and ginger in a very large saucepan. Season well and add enough water to just cover the chicken, about 3 litres. Bring to the boil then simmer for 1 hour.
2 Remove everything from the pan, leaving only the stock. Discard the herbs and ginger and, once it's cool enough to touch, shred the chicken.
3 Meanwhile, return the stock to the boil and add the sherry, saffron and a splash of ginger vinegar, if you have some. Add the pasta and continue to boil until it's almost cooked. To serve, return the shredded chicken and vegetables to the pan and simmer over a low heat until everything is warmed through and the pasta is cooked.
Note Sweet ginger vinegar can be found at Gary Boyce Butchers and Delicatessen (01366 728512), or online at garyboycebutchers.co.uk. It adds a lovely warmth and depth to cocktails, soups and salad dressings.

"MATURE AND ATTRACTIVE (AND DELICIOUS ON A CRACKER)"

CASTELLO® RESERVE HERRGÅRD® • This full-bodied buttery cheese is studded with intense invigorating crystals that leave your taste buds tingling through the night. Consider it a wake-up call to the senses. And a delicious one at that. Best served with red onion marmalade, washed down with champagne and an endless supply of conversation.

HOUSE OF
CASTELLO®
SINCE 1893

PASTA AND RICE

BROWN SHRIMP & PEA PASTA

2 Meanwhile, combine the crushed garlic, minced beef and pork, eggs, pine nuts, parsley and parmesan in a bowl. Squeeze the water out of the bread and break the bread into the bowl. Season and mix well, using your hands, then wet your hands and roll the mixture into portions the size of walnuts.
3 Heat a drizzle of olive oil in a large pan over a medium heat. When the oil is very hot (to prevent the meatballs sticking), carefully add the meatballs and cook, in batches if necessary, for 6-8 minutes, gently moving them about the pan so they brown all over. Add more oil if they begin to stick. Once browned and cooked through, transfer the meatballs to the tomato sauce and leave to simmer.
4 Meanwhile, cook the pasta in a large pan of salted boiling water according to the packet instructions. Drain, then add to the meatballs and tomato sauce. Combine thoroughly and sprinkle with extra parmesan before serving.

BROWN SHRIMP & PEA PASTA

Serves 2
- 200g fettuccine
- 150g frozen peas
- 50g butter
- 2-3 garlic cloves, crushed
- 100g brown shrimps
- Grated zest and juice of 1 lemon
- A small bunch of mint, leaves picked and chopped

1 Cook the pasta in salted boiling water according to packet instructions, then drain, reserving a little cooking water.
2 Meanwhile, boil the peas for 2-3 minutes until just cooked. In a pan, cook the garlic in most of the butter over a medium heat until lightly golden, then add the shrimps, peas and zest. Cook for 1 minute then set aside. Add pasta, mint, lemon juice and remaining butter, then toss and season. Adjust the consistency with the reserved water if need be.

SPAGHETTI & MEATBALLS

Give this classic a lift with a lighter tomato sauce and lots of basil.
Serves 8-10
- 4 garlic cloves (2 finely sliced, 2 crushed)
- Olive oil
- 2 x 400g tins cherry tomatoes
- 500g beef mince
- 500g pork mince
- 2 eggs, beaten
- 2 handfuls of pine nuts, toasted
- 4 tbsp chopped parsley
- 80-100g grated parmesan, plus extra to serve
- 50g stale bread, soaked in warm water for a couple of minutes
- 1kg spaghetti

1 Gently sauté the sliced garlic in a large pan with a drizzle of olive oil. Once the garlic starts to colour, add the tomatoes, season well and leave to simmer.

MOZZARELLA & TOMATO SPAGHETTI

Not pictured
Serves 4
- 400g spaghetti
- 500g ripe tomatoes, peeled and finely chopped
- 2 garlic cloves, chopped
- 1 tsp dried oregano
- 6 tbsp olive oil
- 20 black olives, stoned
- 1 x 200g ball of mozzarella, torn
- 4 anchovy fillets, roughly chopped
- 2 tbsp capers
- 3 basil sprigs, leaves picked, larger ones chopped

1 Cook the spaghetti in salted boiling water according to packet instructions until al dente. Meanwhile, combine all the other ingredients, except the basil leaves, in a bowl to marinate. You can do this while the pasta is cooking but the longer you leave it to marinate, the more the flavours will develop.
2 Drain the pasta. Add to the tomato mixture with the basil leaves and toss well to combine. Serve immediately.

KIDS
LOVE IT

Get your fill

Cannelloni has endless variations. Fill pasta tubes with leftover stew, then cover with any extra stew mixed with tomato sauce, and sprinkle with cheddar. Pureé roasted squash, basil and a little feta, and pipe in; cover with a pesto-béchamel. In autumn, fried mushrooms and bacon with mascarpone, parsley and parmesan is a good filling; while smashed broad beans with ricotta, pecorino and mint is lovely in spring. Mix some white and smoked fish, prawns and herbs into a cheesy béchamel and use to fill the pasta; cover with more sauce, and sprinkle with breadcrumbs to crisp up. If you can't pipe the filling in, use a knife or teaspoon, and a bit of patience.

golden and the pasta tender (if the top browns too fast, cover the dish with foil). Remove from the oven and leave to stand for a few minutes before serving, scattered with the remaining basil.

SPINACH & RICOTTA CANNELLONI

Serves 6

- 400g spinach
- Extra-virgin olive oil
- ¼ tsp ground nutmeg
- 1 onion, diced
- 2 garlic cloves, squashed
- 2 x 400g tins tomatoes
- 1 bay leaf
- ½ bunch of basil, leaves picked
- Grated zest of ½ lemon
- 250g ricotta
- 1 egg, beaten
- 2 tsp grated parmesan
- 150g cannelloni, about 14
- 2 x 125g mozzarella balls, sliced

1 Preheat the oven to 180C/gas 4. Put the spinach and a drizzle of olive oil in a large pan over a low heat. Add the nutmeg, season with salt and pepper, cover and leave to sweat, stirring occasionally, until the spinach has cooked down. Transfer to a bowl and leave to one side to cool a little.
2 In the same pan, heat a drizzle of olive oil and gently cook the onion until soft. Add the garlic, tomatoes, bay leaf, a few basil leaves and the lemon zest. Simmer gently for 20 minutes, until thickened and broken down, then season.
3 Squeeze the moisture out of the spinach, into the bowl. Place the spinach on a board and chop it up, then return to the bowl with the liquid. Stir in the ricotta, beaten egg and parmesan. Season to taste. Sit the piping bag in a jug, fold its edges over the rim, then spoon in the spinach mixture. Pipe the mixture into the cannelloni tubes and lay them in a 20cm x 25cm ovenproof dish.
4 Spread the tomato mixture over the cannelloni. Scatter over most of the remaining basil, lay the mozzarella slices on top, drizzle with extra-virgin olive oil and season. Place in the oven and cook for 35-40 minutes or until the top is

AUBERGINE & TOMATO PASTA

Serves 4-6

- 4-6 tbsp olive oil
- 1 small onion, finely chopped
- 2 garlic cloves, finely chopped
- A small bunch of basil, leaves picked, stalks finely chopped
- 1 x 400g tin chopped tomatoes
- 2 aubergines, cut into 2cm slices
- 500g rigatoni
- 80g ricotta

1 Heat 3 tablespoons of olive oil in a pan and sweat the onion, garlic and basil stalks for 7 minutes. Add the tomatoes, season well and bring to a steady simmer. Cook for about 20 minutes.
2 Meanwhile, fry the aubergines in the remaining oil until golden, then stir into the tomato sauce with most of the basil leaves, reserving a few to garnish.
3 Cook the pasta in salted boiling water according to packet instructions. Drain, then stir through the sauce. To serve, crumble over the ricotta and garnish with the remaining basil leaves.

INDIVIDUAL VEGETARIAN LASAGNES

INDIVIDUAL VEGETARIAN LASAGNES

One of the secrets to good lasagne is to precook your pasta, even if the packet instructions say it's not required. You can use this recipe to make one large lasagne, adjusting the cooking time as required.

Serves 4

- 1.2kg cherry tomatoes, halved
- 5 thyme sprigs, leaves picked
- Extra-virgin olive oil
- 2 shallots, finely chopped
- 2 garlic cloves, crushed to a paste with a little salt
- 500g baby spinach
- 8-12 fresh or dried lasagne sheets
- 350g ricotta

White sauce

- 600ml milk
- 25g butter
- 2 heaped tbsp flour
- 150g vegetarian sharp, mature hard cheese, grated
- 100g vegetarian mozzarella, torn

1 Preheat the oven to 170C/gas 3 and line a shallow baking tray with baking paper. Place the tomatoes, cut-side up, on the tray, sprinkle over the thyme leaves, drizzle with 4 tablespoons of olive oil and season. Place in the oven to roast for 1 hour 15 minutes, until the tomatoes start to caramelise.

2 Meanwhile, prepare the rest of the lasagne. Heat a large frying pan and add a few drops of olive oil. Add the chopped shallots and cook for 5 minutes until soft. Stir in the crushed garlic and cook for another minute, then remove the shallots and garlic from the pan, put in a large bowl and set aside.

3 Use tongs to add the spinach to the pan in 3 batches, and sauté over a high heat until just wilted. Using the tongs, squeeze out as much liquid as possible and discard. Add the spinach to the shallot mixture, toss well and season with pepper. Set aside to cool.

4 For the white sauce, heat the milk in a large saucepan to just below boiling point, then pour into a jug. Wipe out the pan, return to a medium heat and add the butter. Once melted, stir in the flour and cook for 1-2 minutes. Remove from the heat and gradually whisk in the hot

STORE CUPBOARD SUPPER

MARMITE PASTA

milk until you have a smooth sauce. Return the sauce to a medium heat and cook until thickened - it shouldn't be super thick. Off the heat, stir in half the hard cheese and half the mozzarella. Taste, and adjust the seasoning if necessary.

5 Bring a large pan of water to the boil and blanch the lasagne sheets, 2 at a time, for 2 minutes if fresh, 6 minutes if dried. Plunge into a bowl of ice-cold water, then drain on paper towel.

6 Preheat the oven to 180C/gas 4 and start assembling the lasagnes. Drizzle 1-2 tablespoons of white sauce into four 300-350ml ramekins or single-serve pie dishes that are 5-7.5cm deep. Top with a sheet of lasagne; trim to fit if required. Scatter over a few roasted tomatoes, a little spinach and some crumbled ricotta. Repeat with another 2-3 layers of white sauce, lasagne, tomatoes, spinach and ricotta, finishing with sauce. Scatter over the remaining

hard cheese and mozzarella, and place on a baking tray. Bake for 30 minutes, until golden brown and bubbling. Allow the lasagnes to stand for 10 minutes before serving.

MARMITE PASTA

Serves 2

- 200g tagliatelle
- A knob of butter
- 1-2 tsp Marmite
- 40g finely grated parmesan

1 Cook the pasta in salted boiling water according to the packet instructions. Drain, reserving a little cooking water. Return the pan to a low heat and stir in the butter, 1 teaspoon Marmite and most of the parmesan. Stir in enough cooking water so the sauce coats the spaghetti. Turn off the heat. Add more Marmite if needed, then sprinkle over the remaining parmesan to serve.

COURGETTE CARBONARA

GNOCCHI WITH MUSTARDY LEEKS & BACON

COURGETTE CARBONARA

Serves 2

- 200g linguine
- 2 tbsp olive oil
- 1 onion, diced
- 1 garlic clove, chopped
- A small bunch of thyme, leaves picked
- 4 baby courgettes, thinly sliced
- 2 eggs
- 80g grated vegetarian hard cheese

1 Cook the linguine in salted boiling water according to packet instructions. Drain, reserving some of the cooking water, and set aside.
2 Meanwhile, heat the olive oil in a pan and sauté the onion, garlic and thyme for a few minutes until softened. Add the courgettes, season well and cook gently for a few more minutes until tender.
3 Beat the eggs with a handful of cheese and a little pepper. Add the linguine to the courgettes, then pour in the egg mixture, plus a little of the reserved cooking water. Mix until the eggs are just cooked. Serve immediately, topped with the remaining cheese.

GNOCCHI WITH MUSTARDY LEEKS & BACON

Serves 2

- Olive oil
- A knob of butter (optional)
- 2 garlic cloves, finely sliced
- 400g leeks, trimmed, washed, sliced into 1cm rounds
- A few thyme sprigs, leaves picked
- 4 rashers streaky bacon, chopped
- 1 tbsp wholegrain mustard
- 4 tbsp crème fraîche
- 200g gnocchi
- Grated parmesan, to serve

1 Heat a good drizzle of oil, and butter if using, in a large pan over a medium heat. Add the garlic and fry for 1 minute, until golden. Stir in the leeks and thyme, season, then sauté over a low heat for 15 minutes, stirring often, till the leeks turn sticky and soft without colouring.
2 Remove from the pan, add more oil and fry the bacon until crisp. Add mustard, a splash of water and the leeks, and cook for another minute. Add the crème fraîche, bring to the boil, then turn down the heat and simmer.
3 Meanwhile, cook the gnocchi in a large pan of salted boiling water according to the packet instructions. Drain and stir into the leek mixture. Serve the gnocchi topped with grated parmesan.

PRAWN PAD THAI

Serves 2

- 2 tbsp groundnut oil
- 1 red chilli, chopped
- 1 garlic clove, chopped
- 2.5cm piece of ginger, finely chopped
- 4 spring onions, shredded
- 150g green beans, chopped
- A handful of beansprouts
- 180g prawns, peeled
- 1 tsp shrimp paste
- 50g peanuts, chopped
- 150g rice noodles, soaked in hot water till soft, drained
- 1 egg, beaten
- Juice of 1 lime
- A splash each of fish and soy sauce
- A bunch of coriander, chopped

1 In a wok, heat the groundnut oil over a high heat, add the chilli, garlic, ginger and half the spring onions and stir-fry till the onions start to soften. Add the beans, beansprouts, prawns and shrimp paste and cook till the prawns are opaque. Stir in half the peanuts, then the rice noodles, till well combined.
2 When it's all heated, push to one side of the wok and add the egg to the other. Stir until the egg is cooked, then break it up and mix in. Add the lime juice and fish and soy sauces, mix through, and serve immediately topped with the chopped coriander and remaining peanuts.

PRAWN PAD THAI

SQUASH PASTA

SQUASH PASTA

Serves 4

- 400g penne
- ½ butternut squash, cut into 1cm chunks
- 4 tbsp olive oil
- 3 garlic cloves, chopped
- A handful of sage leaves, chopped
- 1 red chilli, deseeded and sliced
- 30g pine nuts, toasted
- Grated parmesan, to serve

1 Cook the pasta in salted boiling water according to the packet instructions, then drain. Meanwhile, cook the squash in a pan of boiling water for 3–4 minutes until almost cooked and drain that, too.
2 Heat the oil in a pan and fry the garlic, sage and chilli until the garlic begins to colour. Add the squash, season, and cook over a medium heat until soft. Toss the pasta in the sauce and sprinkle with the pine nuts and grated parmesan to serve.

CRAB RIGATONI WITH FENNEL & LEMON SALAD

This recipe celebrates all that is delicious about crab, and if you buy picked crabmeat, then making it will be super speedy. The combined sweetness of the crab and tomatoes is a great flavour match for the fresh, aniseedy kick of the fennel.

Serves 4–6

- Olive oil
- 2 large fennel bulbs
- 4 garlic cloves, finely sliced
- 1 bunch of flat-leaf parsley, stalks finely chopped
- 1 tsp dried chilli flakes
- ½ tsp ground cinnamon
- 1 tsp fennel seeds
- 2 lemons
- 2 x 400g tins chopped tomatoes
- 250g cherry tomatoes on the vine
- 500g rigatoni
- 250g brown crabmeat
- 250g white crabmeat

CRAB RIGATONI WITH FENNEL & LEMON SALAD

1 Place a frying pan over a medium heat and add a good glug of olive oil. Peel and finely chop the outer layers of the fennel. Set the leafy tops and inner hearts aside to make a salad later. Add the chopped fennel and garlic to the pan and cook for 2–3 minutes, or until soft.
2 Add the parsley stalks, chilli flakes, cinnamon and fennel seeds to the pan and fry for 2–3 minutes, until it smells fantastic. Finely grate in the zest from your 2 lemons (reserve the lemons) and add the tinned tomatoes. Sit the cherry tomatoes, vines and all, on top to poach. Cover, reduce the heat to low and leave to simmer for 15 minutes.
3 Meanwhile, cook the rigatoni in salted water according to packet instructions.
4 While the pasta and sauce are cooking away, crack on with the salad. Push the reserved fennel hearts and one of the zested lemons through the thinnest slicing attachment on a food processor – or use a mandolin (or a knife, slicing as thinly as you can). Tip into a bowl and season with a good pinch of salt and pepper. Add the reserved fennel tops and gently toss with your fingers. Put aside until you're ready to serve.
5 Check the tomato sauce – it should look rich and glossy and the tomatoes should be soft and squashy. Carefully pick out and discard the vine, leaving the tomatoes in the pan. Gently stir in the brown crabmeat and let it heat up.
6 Drain the rigatoni, reserving a cupful of the cooking water, then gently fold it through the ragù with the white crabmeat, adding a little of the reserved pasta water to loosen the sauce if you think it needs it.
7 Serve the crab pasta on a lovely big platter with the fennel salad bang on top, so you can mix and toss the two together as you serve. Chop the remaining lemon into wedges and serve on the side for squeezing over. The mix of flavours is a knockout!

VEGETARIAN

PEA, MINT & BASIL ARANCINI CAKES

Rice, rice, baby

Risotto accommodates many ingredients - just stir them in at the end, after using the basic method below (omitting the squash and pancetta). Try adding chopped pear and gorgonzola, and top with toasted walnuts. For cauliflower risotto, add cooked florets; for a spicy topping, fry anchovies till melted, then add chilli flakes and breadcrumbs, and cook till crisp. For a vegetarian option, fry off field or wild mushrooms after the onions, then add the rice, and use veg stock instead of chicken. In summer, all you need is ripe tomatoes, basil and lots of parmesan. Or, add thinly sliced raw squid near the end of cooking and halve the cheese; when the squid is cooked, finish with chopped chilli, parsley and lemon juice. To use up leftovers, place in a dish and bake until golden and heated through; slice and serve with an apéritif.

BUTTERNUT SQUASH & PANCETTA RISOTTO

PEA, MINT & BASIL ARANCINI CAKES

Serves 4

- 5 spring onions, finely chopped
- 1 tbsp olive oil
- 1 small garlic clove, finely chopped
- 160g arborio rice
- 80ml white wine
- 500ml hot vegetable stock
- 40g frozen peas
- 20g butter
- 20g strong, hard vegetarian cheese
- Grated zest of 1 lemon, plus a squeeze of juice
- 2 mint sprigs, leaves chopped
- ½ bunch of basil, leaves chopped
- 2 eggs, beaten
- 200g breadcrumbs
- Vegetable oil, for frying

1 Gently fry half the spring onions in the oil until soft. Add the garlic and cook for 1 minute. Increase the heat, add the rice and stir for 2 minutes until translucent.

2 Add the wine and keep stirring until it has been absorbed. Add the hot stock in small amounts, stirring continuously over a low heat until the rice is almost cooked; you may not need all the stock. Add the peas and cook for 2-3 minutes.
3 Off the heat, stir in the butter, cheese, remaining spring onions, zest, herbs and seasoning. Leave to cool completely.
4 Shape small handfuls into cakes. Dip into the egg, then coat in breadcrumbs. Fill a large frying pan with oil, halfway up the cakes, then fry them for 3-4 minutes each side until golden; drain on kitchen paper. Serve with a squeeze of lemon.

BUTTERNUT SQUASH & PANCETTA RISOTTO

Serves 2

- 4 pancetta rashers
- 1 tbsp olive oil
- 150g butternut squash, diced
- 3 thyme sprigs
- 25g butter
- 1 small onion, finely diced
- 1 garlic clove, finely chopped
- 140g risotto rice
- 100ml white wine
- 750ml chicken stock
- 40g parmesan, grated

1 Fry the pancetta in the oil until crisp, then break into shards. Fry the squash and thyme in the pan until the squash is turning golden. Add a little water, lower the heat and cook until tender; set aside.
2 Meanwhile, melt the butter in a wide pan and sweat the onion and garlic until translucent. Add the rice, cook for 1-2 minutes, then add the wine. When it's reduced right down, add stock, 1 ladle at a time, stirring till absorbed before adding more. When the rice is almost cooked, stir in squash and most of the pancetta. When the rice is done, stir in most of the cheese. Season, then serve topped with remaining meat and cheese.

JEWELLED RICE

ALL-IN-ONE RICE & CHICKEN

JEWELLED RICE

This exotic side dish promises crisp onions, dried cherries and pistachio nuts in every bite.

Serves 4-6

- 300g red, wild, brown or basmati rice, or a mixture
- A knob of butter
- 3 red onions, finely sliced
- 1 x 410g tin lentils, drained
- 75g pistachios, chopped
- 100g dried sour cherries or dried cranberries, chopped
- Juice of 2 lemons
- A large bunch of mint, leaves picked and roughly chopped
- A large bunch of coriander, leaves picked and roughly chopped
- Walnut or extra-virgin olive oil

1 Cook the rice according to the packet instructions. Meanwhile, melt the butter in a large nonstick frying pan over a low heat. Add the onions and sauté for 15 minutes, or till caramelised and crisp.
2 Place the lentils in a large bowl with the cooked rice, pistachios, cherries or cranberries and lemon juice, and season well. Add the herbs and a good drizzle of walnut or extra-virgin olive oil, and toss to mix. Top with the crisp onions and serve with grilled meat or fish.

ALL-IN-ONE RICE & CHICKEN

Serves 4

- 2 chicken legs and 2 thighs
- Olive oil
- 1 onion, diced
- 1 garlic clove, crushed
- 2 tsp ground coriander
- 1 heaped tsp cumin
- 50g long-grain rice
- 150g medjool dates, chopped
- 1 tbsp honey

1 Season the chicken pieces, then heat a glug of olive oil in a large pan and brown them. Remove the chicken and set aside. In the same pan, sweat the diced onion over a medium heat until softened, then add the garlic, ground coriander and cumin. Cook for 2 minutes then add the rice, dates and honey.
2 Return the chicken to the pan and mix well. Cover with water and add a little salt. Bring to the boil, then leave the mixture to simmer, covered, over a medium heat for 30 minutes till the rice and chicken are cooked. Season and serve with salad or greens.

PERSIAN RICE & LAMB

Serves 6-8

- 1 onion, sliced
- 2 large knobs of butter
- 750g lamb neck fillet, cut in 3cm pieces
- A good pinch of saffron
- 2 tsp cardamom pods, crushed and seeds removed (pods discarded)
- 1 cinnamon stick
- 2 tsp cumin
- 3 tomatoes, skinned and chopped
- 2 litres hot vegetable stock
- 2 large waxy potatoes, such as charlotte or maris peer, finely sliced
- 500g basmati rice
- Pomegranate and parsley, to serve

1 Fry the onion in half the butter in a heavy pan. Add the lamb and brown all over. Season, add spices and tomatoes. Cover the meat with stock. Simmer, covered, for about 1 hour, till tender; stir occasionally. Add more stock if needed.
2 Melt the remaining butter in a wide saucepan. Add the potato in 1 layer. Fry over a medium heat for 5 minutes, or till crisping up. Add two-thirds of the rice, then the lamb stew and remaining rice; season. Add stock to cover it all by 2cm. Cover, bring to the boil then simmer for 15 minutes. Uncover and cook for 5-10 minutes to crisp the bottom. Serve on a platter scattered with pomegranate seeds and chopped parsley.

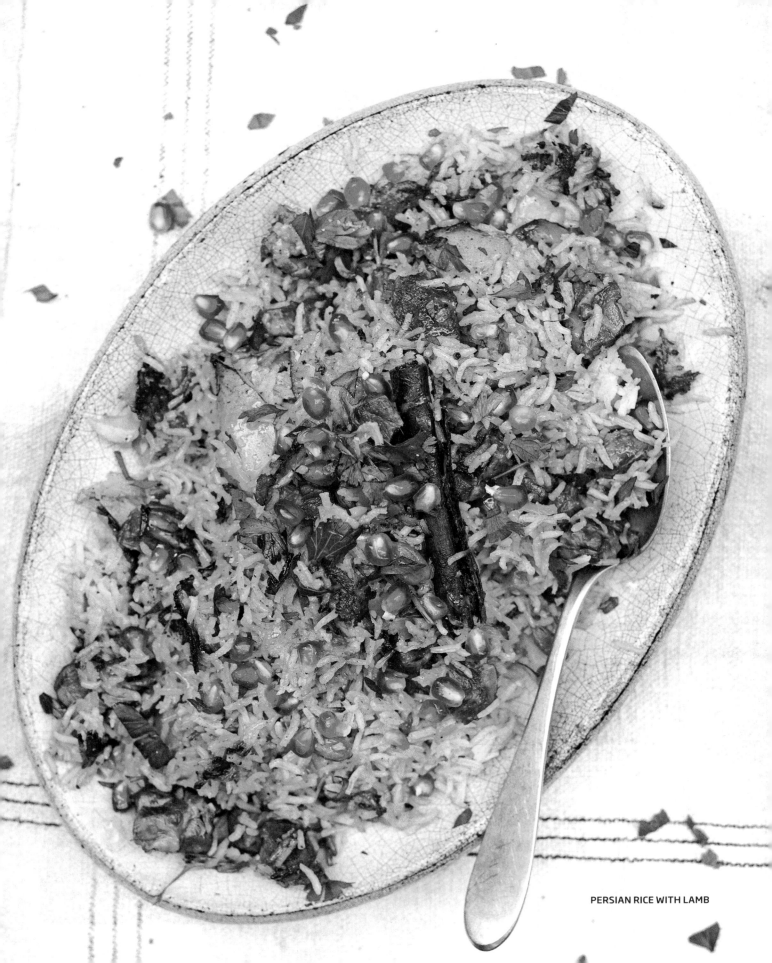

PERSIAN RICE WITH LAMB

GB

JAMIE OLIVER FOOD GUIDE

OVER 1000 LOCATIONS TO EAT, SHOP AND VISIT

SALAD AND VEG

ASIAN-STYLE WATERMELON SALAD

ASIAN-STYLE WATERMELON SALAD

Watermelon is so refreshing – and with fresh mint, radishes and the dressing's ginger-chilli hum, it's a stunning salad.

Serves 6-8 as a starter or side

- 20g sesame seeds
- ½ watermelon, flesh scooped out and cut into 1cm chunks
- 1 bunch of breakfast radishes, any nice tops left on, finely sliced
- ½ bunch of mint, finely sliced, baby leaves reserved
- Lime wedges, to serve (optional)

Spicy dressing

- ½ garlic clove
- A thumb-sized piece of ginger
- 1-2 red chillies, seeded
- 1 tbsp soy sauce
- 1 tbsp sesame oil
- Juice of 2 limes

1 Toast the sesame seeds in a hot pan over a medium-high heat for a couple of minutes until they're golden and smelling fantastic. Set aside.
2 For the dressing, finely grate the garlic, ginger and chillies into a clean jam jar. Add the rest of the dressing ingredients, put the lid on the jar and shake well to combine.
3 Combine the watermelon chunks and radishes in a bowl, pour over the dressing, scatter over the sliced mint and toss to combine. Finish off with a scattering of toasted sesame seeds and the baby mint leaves, and serve with lime wedges if you like.

WARM BAKED PEAR SALAD

Frisée is quite an under-used lettuce, but the slightly bitter leaves are so delicious when combined with something sweet, like gorgeous soft pears and sticky maple pecans.

Serves 6 as a starter

- 3 ripe pears, peeled, cored and quartered
- 6 rashers of good-quality smoked streaky bacon
- 2 tbsp maple syrup
- 75g pecans
- 1 frisée lettuce
- 2 x 20g punnets of mixed baby cress
- 1 bag of watercress

Mustard dressing

- ½ tsp wholegrain mustard
- Juice of ½ lemon
- Extra-virgin olive oil

1 Preheat the oven to 190C/gas 5. Pop the pears in a small roasting tray and drape the bacon over the top. Cook in the oven for 10 minutes then drizzle over the maple syrup, add the pecans and jiggle the tray to coat everything. Return the tray to the oven for another 15-20 minutes, until the pears are soft and sweet, the nuts slightly toasted and caramelised and the bacon crispy.
2 Meanwhile, get rid of any tatty outer leaves from the lettuce, then snap off the larger dark leaves and save them for another day. Wash the pale inner leaves, dry in a salad spinner and place in a serving dish. Snip the mixed cress over the top and add the watercress.
3 Combine the dressing ingredients in a small cup or jar and take to the table with the salad. Make sure everyone is round the table, then toss the salad leaves with the dressing, soft pears, toasted nuts and crispy bacon and get into it immediately.

WEEKEND
LUNCH

WARM BAKED PEAR SALAD

MANDOLIN SALAD

GINGER & GARLIC GREENS

JOOLS'S CHOPPED SALAD

MANDOLIN SALAD

The beauty of mandolins, as you'll see in this simple salad, is that they quickly turn inherently frumpy things into things of beauty.

Serves 6 as a starter or side

- 200g soft goat's cheese
- 50ml milk
- 3 large raw beetroots, different colours if possible, such as golden, candy and red, peeled and trimmed
- 2 apples
- Rapeseed oil
- Cider vinegar
- ½ bunch of mint, leaves picked and finely sliced

1 Whizz the goat's cheese and milk in a food processor until blended to the consistency of thick cream. Season to taste then spoon over a large platter.
2 Finely slice the beetroots and apples (cores and all) using a mandolin. Toss them together with a little drizzle of rapeseed oil and a tiny splash of cider vinegar. Pile it all on top of the goat's cheese, sprinkle over the mint and serve immediately.

GINGER & GARLIC GREENS

Serves 4

- 2 tbsp groundnut oil
- 2-3 garlic cloves, thinly sliced
- A thumb-sized piece of ginger, cut into matchsticks
- 350g Chinese greens (such as bok choi or choi sum)
- 1 tbsp soy sauce
- 1 tbsp sesame oil

1 Heat the groundnut oil in a wok or large pan until very hot. Add the garlic and ginger and cook over a high heat for 1-2 minutes, stirring frequently, until fragrant and turning golden.
2 Add the greens, soy and a splash of water, and stir-fry until the greens are cooked through. Remove from the heat, stir in the sesame oil and serve.

JOOLS'S CHOPPED SALAD

This is the clever way my wife, Jools, gets all our kids - even the babies - to eat lots of salad. Everything is chopped extra fine and tiny, almost like a salsa, making it an absolute pleasure to eat.

Serves 4-6 as a side

- 6 small carrots, mixed if possible
- 2 celery stalks, trimmed
- A handful of mixed cherry tomatoes
- 2 little gem lettuces
- 100g feta
- A few mint sprigs, leaves picked
- 1 tbsp balsamic vinegar
- 3 tbsp extra-virgin olive oil

1 Finely chop the carrots, celery, cherry tomatoes and lettuces separately on a large board. Once everything is fairly fine, start mixing it all together and chopping some more.
2 Crumble over the feta cheese, then roll up the mint leaves, like a cigar, and chop them into the salad.
3 Combine the balsamic vinegar and extra-virgin olive oil with a pinch of salt and pepper in a jam jar. Take the board of salad to the table with the dressing and dress just before eating.

LEEKS WITH MUSTARD & DILL VINAIGRETTE & FETA

Classy dresser

You can't beat homemade coleslaw and there are lots of ways to bring the classic shredded cabbage, carrot, onion and mayo combo to life. If you like punchy slaw, try stirring in dijon mustard, horseradish sauce or even wasabi. Add fragrance by introducing chopped herbs, or different textures with shredded apple and crushed salted almonds. A slaw made with maple syrup, pecans and a dash of vinegar is great with grilled meat. Swap out the usual veg in favour of asparagus, courgettes and fennel and drizzle with an anchovy dressing. Shred yard-long or runner beans, toss in fish sauce, sugar and vinegar and sprinkle with chopped tomatoes and peanuts for a Thai version.

EASY SLAW
Not pictured
Serves 4
- 1 carrot
- 1 red onion
- A handful of kale
- ½ white cabbage
- 2 tbsp mayonnaise
- 50g dried figs, chopped
- Juice of ½ lemon
- A handful of chopped parsley

1 Finely slice the veg or use the julienne slicer on a food processor. Combine with mayonnaise, figs and juice. Season and stir through the parsley. Serve as a side.

TOMATO & MINT SALAD
Not pictured
Serves 4
- 400g tomatoes, chopped
- ½ red onion, finely sliced
- Grated zest and juice of ½ lemon
- 2 mint sprigs, leaves picked and finely chopped

1 Mix everything together in a bowl and season with salt and pepper. Marinate for about 10 minutes before transferring to a platter to serve.

LEEKS WITH MUSTARD & DILL VINAIGRETTE & FETA
Serves 2
- 350g young leeks
- 1 tsp dijon mustard
- 1 small garlic clove, crushed
- 2 tbsp olive oil
- 2 tsp lemon juice
- 1 tbsp chopped dill
- 30g feta

1 Get a pan that's large enough to hold the leeks in a single flat layer, and add about 2cm water. Bring to the boil, add the leeks, then cover and simmer for 4–5 minutes until tender. Drain, then refresh the leeks under a cold tap.
2 Whisk the dijon, garlic, olive oil and lemon juice together in a small bowl. Stir in the dill and season to taste.
3 Arrange the leeks in a serving dish and pour over dressing. Crumble the feta over the top and serve.

FENNEL, CRAB & ORANGE SALAD
Serves 2
- 1 fennel bulb
- 1½ oranges, 1 peeled and sliced; ½ juiced
- 100g white crabmeat
- 2 mint sprigs, leaves torn
- 1 avocado, peeled, stoned and sliced
- ½ green chilli, diced
- 2 tbsp extra-virgin olive oil

1 Thinly slice the fennel on a mandolin, or using a very sharp knife, and refresh in a bowl of iced water. Arrange the orange slices on a serving platter with the drained fennel, crabmeat, mint, sliced avocado and chilli.
2 Make a dressing by whisking the orange juice together with the olive oil, or shaking in a jam jar until combined, and season generously with salt and pepper. Drizzle the dressing over the salad and serve at once.

FENNEL, CRAB & ORANGE SALAD

VEGETARIAN

SPINACH & PANEER PATTIES WITH MINT YOGHURT

ASIAN SMASH

ANCHOIADE BOUZIGODE

SPINACH & PANEER PATTIES WITH MINT YOGHURT

Serves 4

- Groundnut oil
- 3 garlic cloves, sliced
- 5cm piece of ginger, grated
- 1 green chilli, seeded and sliced
- ½ tsp garam masala
- ½ tsp each ground coriander, cumin and turmeric
- 100g spinach, chopped
- ½ bunch of coriander, leaves picked and finely chopped
- 1 maris piper potato, cooked, mashed
- 225g paneer, grated (see note)
- 2 tbsp chickpea flour
- 1 tsp baking powder
- ½ lemon
- Naan and mango chutney, to serve

Mint yoghurt

- A few mint sprigs, leaves picked and finely chopped
- 150g plain yoghurt

1 Place a nonstick pan over a medium heat and add a drizzle of groundnut oil. Add the garlic, ginger and chilli and fry for 1 minute. Add the garam masala and ground spices, fry for another minute then add the spinach and coriander leaves. Reduce the heat and cook until the spinach is wilted. Leave to cool.

2 Combine the mashed potato in a large bowl with the spinach, paneer, chickpea flour, baking powder and a squeeze of lemon juice. Season well and form into 4–5cm patties. Firm up in the fridge for at least 30 minutes, then barbecue the patties for 3-4 minutes each side until charred and cooked through.

3 For the mint yoghurt, stir the mint through the yoghurt. To serve, heat the naan on the barbecue, then top with the patties, mint yoghurt and chutney.

Note Paneer is an unsalted curd cheese common in Indian cooking. Buy from Asian grocers or major supermarkets.

ASIAN SMASH

Serves 4-6

- 3 sweet potatoes, chopped
- 4 desiree potatoes, chopped
- 4 carrots, chopped
- ½ large swede, chopped
- Olive oil
- 4 garlic cloves, sliced
- 2.5cm piece of ginger, cut into matchsticks
- 1 red chilli, deseeded and sliced
- ½ bunch of coriander, leaves picked and stalks chopped
- ½ tsp mustard seeds
- ½ tsp turmeric
- 50g butter

1 Cook the vegetables in boiling salted water for 12-15 minutes, till soft.

2 Meanwhile, heat a little oil in a pan and fry the garlic, ginger and chilli until soft, about 1 minute. Stir in the coriander stalks, mustard seeds and turmeric, then remove from heat.

3 Drain the vegetables, then steam dry a little and return to the pan. Coarsely mash with the butter, spices, salt and pepper. Sprinkle with coriander leaves before serving.

ANCHOIADE BOUZIGODE

Recipe by Caroline Conran, Le Marin restaurant
Serves 6

- 2 large, firm tomatoes, sliced
- 3-4 spring onions, cut into quarters
- 2 green peppers, preferably long, grilled, skinned and cut into thin strips
- 12 anchovy fillets in oil, drained
- 2 tbsp black olives, stoned
- 6 hard-boiled eggs, halved
- Extra-virgin olive oil

1 Arrange the tomatoes in a serving dish. Scatter over the spring onions, peppers and anchovies. Dot with the black olives, then arrange the eggs on top. Lightly drizzle with the oil to serve.

SPRING PIE

Pie chart

A filo pastry base is all you need to create a whole range of delicious pies. In winter, try combining kale and onions, then pour over a mixture of crème fraîche, egg yolk and grated parmesan and top with anchovies and black olives. In autumn, try roasted squash topped with torn chunks of goat's cheese, or wild mushrooms cooked with thyme and parsley. Scatter the top with parmesan once it comes out of the oven. In summer, fill your pie with roasted aubergines, red peppers and tomatoes and drizzle generously with pesto. Or grill thin strips of courgette, grate over lemon zest and tear over basil leaves before topping with dollops of ricotta and a little olive oil. Fruit works well too. Try berries, plums or sliced apple covered in homemade thick custard, sprinkled with sugar and baked till golden.

SPRING PIE

Serves 6

- Olive oil
- 270g filo pastry
- 200g baby spinach
- 6 streaky bacon rashers
- 6 eggs
- 200ml milk
- 1 tsp mustard powder
- ½ bunch of chives
- Grated zest of 1 lemon
- 3 medium leeks, sliced
- Green salad, to serve

1 Preheat the oven to 180C/gas 4 and grease a 20cm x 30cm baking dish with olive oil. Cover with a layer of pastry, letting the edges overhang slightly. Brush with a little oil then add another layer of pastry, repeating until you have used it all (there should be 3 or 4 layers). 2 Boil the kettle, then place the spinach in a colander and pour over the hot water to wilt it (you may have to do this in 2 batches). Push the spinach down with the back of a spoon to drain then, when cool enough to handle, squeeze out any excess water with your hands. Transfer the spinach to a board and roughly chop, then place in a large bowl and set aside.
3 Preheat the grill to high and grill the bacon till crisp, then set aside to cool. Whisk the eggs in a large bowl with a pinch of salt and pepper. Whisk in the milk and mustard powder and snip in the chives, then grate in the lemon zest. Crumble the cooled bacon into the bowl of spinach then add the sliced leeks.
4 Mix well to combine, then scatter the vegetable mixture over the pastry case. Pour the egg mixture evenly over the vegetables and carefully place the dish on the bottom of the oven. Bake for 30-40 minutes, or until the pie is just set. Leave the pie to cool in the baking dish for 20 minutes before slicing. Serve warm with a crisp green salad.

BROCCOLI, FETA, RADISH & QUINOA SALAD

Serves 6

- 200g quinoa
- 100g radishes
- 400g purple-sprouting broccoli
- Avocado oil
- 1 tsp sweet smoked paprika
- 1 tsp nigella seeds
- Juice of 2 lemons
- 200g feta, crumbled
- 2 tbsp pumpkin seeds, toasted

1 Cook the quinoa according to the packet instructions and place in a large bowl. Use a speed peeler or mandolin to thinly slice the radishes into the bowl.
2 Put the broccoli in another bowl, drizzle with a little avocado oil, then sprinkle over the paprika and nigella seeds; toss well. Cook on a barbecue or griddle for 10 minutes, turning every few minutes, until lightly charred but still with some bite.
3 Add the broccoli to the quinoa with the lemon juice and a good drizzle of oil, season, and toss. Finish by sprinkling over the feta and the pumpkin seeds.

BROCCOLI, FETA, RADISH & QUINOA SALAD

MELANZANE PARMIGIANA

BLOOD ORANGE & FENNEL SALAD

MELANZANE PARMIGIANA

Serves 2 as a side

- Olive oil
- 1 large (about 275g) aubergine, cut into 1cm-thick slices
- Flour, to coat
- 3 tbsp tomato and basil sauce or tomato passata
- A handful of basil leaves
- 20g grated parmesan
- 1 ball of mozzarella, torn into small pieces

1 Preheat the oven to 190C/gas 5. Heat a deep-fryer of olive oil or add a generous drizzle to a large pan over a high heat. Lightly dust the aubergine slices with a little flour and season well. Carefully fry the aubergine, in batches, on both sides until soft and golden.
2 Lightly oil a shallow 11cm x 18cm baking dish and place a few slices of aubergine on the bottom. Spoon over a little tomato sauce, add a few torn basil leaves, a sprinkle of parmesan and a little mozzarella, and season well. Continue to layer the ingredients, finishing with a layer of mozzarella and parmesan. Place in the hot oven and cook for 15–20 minutes or until bubbling and golden. Garnish with a couple of basil leaves to serve.

BLOOD ORANGE & FENNEL SALAD

Serves 4

- 2 handfuls of almonds
- A drizzle of honey
- 35g rocket
- 35g pea shoots
- A small bunch of mint, leaves picked
- 2 fennel bulbs, tough outer leaves discarded, finely shaved
- 4 blood oranges, peeled and thinly sliced horizontally
- Seeds from ½ pomegranate
- Juice of ½ lemon
- Olive oil
- 40g pecorino, shaved, to serve

1 Preheat the oven to 170C/gas 3. Place the almonds on a baking tray and sprinkle generously with sea salt. Roast for 5 minutes or until golden. While hot, drizzle with honey and toss well.
2 Place the rocket, pea shoots, mint, fennel, orange slices and pomegranate seeds in bowl and season. Squeeze over the lemon juice and drizzle with olive oil. Gently toss, then divide between serving plates and scatter over the pecorino and roasted almonds to serve.

FUNKY & POSH CHIPS

Serves 4

- 4 large floury potatoes (about 300g each), peeled and cut into 1cm-thick chips
- Vegetable oil

Funky chips
- 1 garlic clove, thinly sliced
- A handful of chopped parsley

Posh chips
- A drizzle of truffle oil (combine with olive oil if it's very strong)
- 8g grated parmesan

1 Parboil the chips in salted boiling water for 8-10 minutes until soft but keeping their shape. Drain in a colander and leave to steam until completely dry. This is very important before frying.
2 Heat a deep-fryer to 180C or fill a deep saucepan to three-quarters full with vegetable oil over high heat. For safety, make sure there are no kids around and never leave oil unattended. The oil is hot enough when a cube of bread turns golden in 10 seconds. Carefully fry the chips, in batches, until crisp then drain on kitchen paper and sprinkle with sea salt.
3 If you're feeling funky, carefully mix the hot chips with garlic and parsley; or if posh, drizzle with truffle oil and sprinkle with parmesan. Serve hot.

SUPER SIDE

MUJADARA, GARLIC YOGHURT, AND CARROT & BEETROOT SALAD

MUJADARA, GARLIC YOGHURT, AND CARROT & BEETROOT SALAD

Serves 6

- 120g brown lentils (sometimes called green lentils), rinsed
- 120g basmati rice
- 2 tbsp olive oil
- ½ tbsp ground cumin
- ½ tsp turmeric
- ½ tsp ground cinnamon
- Sunflower oil, for frying
- 1 onion, finely sliced

Carrot & beetroot salad

- 4 small beetroots, skins on
- 300g young chantenay carrots
- 1 small red onion, finely sliced
- 80ml olive oil
- 1 tbsp red wine vinegar
- ¾ tsp ground cumin
- ½ bunch of flat-leaf parsley, leaves chopped

Garlic yoghurt

- 250g thick Greek-style yoghurt
- 1 small garlic clove, crushed
- 1 tbsp olive oil
- ¼ tsp cayenne pepper

1 Rinse the lentils in cold water, then place in a pan and cover with water. Bring to the boil then simmer over a medium heat until tender but still with some bite, about 20 minutes.
2 Meanwhile, wash and drain the rice. Heat the olive oil in a pan over a medium heat and stir in the spices. Add the rice, stirring to coat in the oil and spices. Stir in 225ml water. Turn the heat to very low, cover, and cook for 8 minutes. Turn off the heat and leave for 5 minutes, covered, then fluff the rice with a fork.
3 Heat enough sunflower oil in a pan to cover the surface. Add the onion and fry, stirring occasionally, until crisp and golden. Drain on paper towel.
4 Combine the rice, lentils and half the onion. Season, then place in a serving bowl and top with remaining onion.
5 For the yoghurt, mix with the garlic and season. Pour into a bowl. Drizzle with oil and sprinkle with cayenne.
6 For the salad, simmer the beetroots in water until tender, about 1 hour. When cool, peel and cut into wedges. Simmer the carrots in water until just cooked. Put the beetroots, carrots and red onion in a serving bowl. Combine the

olive oil, vinegar and cumin, season, then pour on the veg. Add the parsley, toss and serve at room temperature with the mujadara and garlic yoghurt.

TOFU & CHICKPEA CURRY WITH GREENS

Serves 4

- 1 tbsp vegetable oil
- 1 red onion, sliced
- 3 garlic cloves, finely chopped
- 1 tbsp ground coriander
- 2 tsp ground cumin
- ½ tsp cayenne pepper
- 1 tsp turmeric
- 1 x 400g tin chopped tomatoes
- 2 tbsp olive oil
- 200g tofu, cut into cubes
- 1 x 400g tin chickpeas, drained and rinsed
- 2 tsp paprika
- 2 tsp garam masala
- Juice of ½ lemon
- 2 tsp cumin seeds
- 1 red chilli, sliced
- 200g spring greens, shredded

1 Heat the vegetable oil in a pan. Add the onion and one-third of the garlic. Cook gently until the onion begins to brown. Add the coriander, cumin, cayenne and turmeric and cook for 1 minute. Stir in the tomatoes and half a tin of water. Simmer for 10 minutes.
2 Meanwhile, heat half the olive oil in a pan and cook the tofu until golden. Drain on paper towel. Stir the chickpeas into the tomato sauce. Heat through, then add the paprika, garam masala and lemon juice. Season. Add water if it looks too dry. Add the tofu.
3 Heat the remaining olive oil in a pan. Add the cumin seeds and fry gently, then add the remaining garlic and chilli. When the garlic begins to brown, add the greens and stir-fry for 2–3 minutes, until just cooked. Serve with the curry.

TOFU & CHICKPEA CURRY WITH GREENS

BARBECUED SPRING VEGETABLES

MEXICAN SWEETCORN SALAD

BARBECUED SPRING VEGETABLES WITH ORANGE DRESSING

Serves 6

- 300g baby carrots, trimmed and halved
- 175g baby leeks, or spring onions, trimmed
- 300g baby courgettes, halved lengthways
- 500g asparagus, trimmed
- 150g green beans, trimmed
- 2 tsp cumin seeds
- ½ tsp dried chilli flakes
- A pinch of ground cinnamon
- Extra-virgin olive oil
- Juice of ½ orange
- 1 x 20g punnet of cress

1 Blanch the carrots and leeks in a pan of salted boiling water for 3 minutes, drain. Place in a large, shallow dish with the courgettes, asparagus, beans, spices and some olive oil. Season and toss.
2 Transfer the veg to a hot barbecue and cook, turning occasionally, for 5-6 minutes, until charred and cooked.
3 Meanwhile, place the orange juice in a large, shallow bowl and add an equal amount of olive oil. As soon as the veg are cooked, plunge them into the dressing and toss to coat. Snip over some cress and serve.

MEXICAN SWEETCORN SALAD

Serves 3-4 as a side

- 2 corn cobs
- ½ green pepper, deseeded
- ½ red pepper, deseeded
- 4 spring onions, trimmed
- ½ green chilli
- ½ bunch each of coriander and mint, leaves picked
- 1 tbsp olive oil
- Juice of 1 lime

1 Cook the corn in salted boiling water for 4-5 minutes until just tender. Drain and leave to cool slightly.
2 Finely chop the peppers, spring onions, chilli, coriander and mint and place in a bowl. Slice the kernels from the cobs and add to the bowl with the rest of the ingredients. Season, drizzle with the oil and lime juice and toss well.

MEXICAN BLACK BEAN BURGERS

Serves 6

- 2 handfuls of rolled oats
- 2 tbsp salted peanuts
- 2 x 400g tins black beans, drained
- 1 red onion, grated
- 1 red chilli, deseeded, finely chopped
- ½ tsp ground coriander
- 1 tsp ground cumin
- ½ bunch of coriander, leaves picked
- Grated zest of 1 lime
- Olive oil
- Flour, for dusting
- 1 tsp sweet smoked paprika
- 6 ciabatta rolls, split
- Baby rocket, tomato salsa, sliced avocado, and lime wedges, to serve

1 Blitz the oats and peanuts in a food processor until coarsely chopped. Add 1½ tins of beans, the onion, chilli, ground coriander and cumin, coriander leaves, lime zest and a good drizzle of olive oil and blitz to combine. Add the remaining beans and pulse just once or twice, so they stay a little chunky. Transfer the mixture to a bowl.
2 Divide into 6 balls then flatten into burgers on a clean surface dusted with flour and smoked paprika. Place on a tray and chill for at least an hour.
3 Preheat a chargrill pan to a high heat. Place the bread, cut-side down, on the grill and cook until lightly charred. Set aside. Cook the bean burgers for 4-5 minutes each side until they are lightly charred and cooked through. Scatter the rocket over 6 roll halves and top with the burgers, salsa, avocado and remaining roll halves. Serve with lime wedges for squeezing.

GET JAMIE ON IPAD!

Jamie Magazine is now available as an iPad app.
The app features all the great content you'd find in the magazine – and more.

Not only do you receive all the recipes, foodie travel guides and snippets and insights into Jamie's life that you get from the printed magazine, but you'll also find bonus photos, previously unseen material and a whole host of interactive features.

You can build up scrapbooks of your top recipes and share your favourites with your friends via Facebook, Twitter and email. You can rate recipes and see which dishes are most popular with other users. You can also pick up back issues for less than it costs to buy the paper equivalent.

FISH AND SEAFOOD

POUTING FISH FINGERS & SWEET POTATO CHIPS

pound the rest with a pinch of salt using a pestle and mortar until you've got a paste. Add the mayonnaise and lemon juice and muddle it together.

5 Serve the pouting with a portion of sweet potato chips, a dollop of basil mayo and a wedge of lemon. Delicious with a green salad or buttered peas.

FISH FINGER BUTTY

This is the treat of all treats – the parmesan crust makes it insanely good. If you get lovely fresh fish, it will be so flaky and juicy made this way that you won't believe it.

Serves 2

- 300–350g pollack or line-caught haddock fillet (skinned and pin-boned)
- 100g matzo crackers or water biscuits
- A small handful of grated parmesan
- 1 bunch of flat-leaf parsley, leaves picked and finely chopped
- Grated zest and juice of 1 lemon
- 1 egg
- Vegetable oil
- 70g tartare sauce (shop-bought is OK)
- 1 tbsp capers
- 4 thick slices of farmhouse loaf
- 2 handfuls of cress
- Lemon wedges, to serve

POUTING FISH FINGERS & SWEET POTATO CHIPS

Pouting is from the same family as cod so makes a great alternative to its over-fished cousin. Use whole fillets, or cut them lengthways for fish fingers.

Serves 2

- 2 x 130g pouting or whiting fillets, skin on, scaled and pin-boned
- 2 heaped tbsp flour
- 1 egg, beaten
- 50g fresh breadcrumbs
- 1 garlic clove, crushed
- A couple of rosemary sprigs
- ½ lemon, cut into wedges

Sweet potato chips

- 2 medium sweet potatoes, scrubbed and cut lengthways into 8 wedges
- ½ tsp sweet smoked paprika
- Olive oil

Basil mayo

- 4 basil sprigs
- 2 heaped tbsp mayonnaise
- Juice of ½ lemon

1 For the sweet potato chips, preheat the oven to 200C/gas 6. In a roasting tray, toss the wedges with salt and pepper, the paprika and a glug of olive oil. Cook in the oven for 35–40 minutes or until golden and cooked through.

2 Coat the fillets with seasoned flour. Dunk them in the beaten egg then transfer to the breadcrumbs and move about until well coated on all sides.

3 Put a large frying pan over a medium heat. Add a glug of olive oil along with the garlic and rosemary to flavour the oil. When the garlic sizzles, shake the fillets to get rid of excess breadcrumbs then add them to the pan, skin-side down. If you're cooking fish fingers, they'll need 5–6 minutes; a fillet 7–8 minutes. Don't touch the fish – use your instincts and let it cook until golden underneath, then flip and reduce the heat while it finishes cooking.

4 Meanwhile, for the mayo, get rid of the tough ends of the basil stalks then

1 Cut the fillet into 6 finger-shaped portions. Blitz the crackers in a food processor until you have fine crumbs, or bash them up in a clean tea towel with a rolling pin. Mix the crumbs with the parmesan, half the parsley, lemon zest, salt and pepper. Place this mixture in a wide bowl or on a plate. Beat the egg in a bowl and place next to the crumbs.

2 Dip the fish into the egg and then drop it into the crumbs. Turn and pat the fish so it is evenly coated. Repeat until you have done all your fish portions.

3 Heat a large frying pan over a medium heat and pour in 1cm oil. When the oil is hot, fry the fish fingers, turning once, for 2–3 minutes each side, until golden and cooked through. Have kitchen towel ready to drain off any excess oil.

4 In a bowl, mix the tartare sauce, capers, a squeeze of lemon juice and the remaining parsley. Spread a layer of tartar on the bread, then the hot fish, then cress. Serve with lemon wedges.

EVERYBODY LOVES IT

FISH FINGER BUTTY

COLEY KORMA WITH FLUFFY RICE

There's loads of coley (also known as saithe and coalfish) in the sea, and it's meaty, sweet and melts in the mouth. It's often half the price of cod, so you could feed twice as many or just save money. Normally you'd start cooking a fillet of fish skin-side down, but I've gone flesh-side down here to encrust the fish and get those flavours going.

Serves 4

- 1 cup basmati rice
- 2 heaped tbsp korma paste
- 4 x 180g coley fillets, skin on, scaled and pin-boned
- Olive oil
- 4 spring onions, finely sliced
- 200ml low-fat coconut milk
- A few coriander sprigs, leaves picked, stalks finely chopped
- ½-1 red chilli, finely sliced
- 1 lemon, cut into wedges

1 Place the rice in a saucepan with 2 mugs of boiling water and a pinch of salt and bring to the boil over a high heat. Cover with a lid, reduce to a low heat and cook for 7–8 minutes.
2 Meanwhile, put a large pan over a medium heat. Spread 1 tablespoon of korma paste all over the flesh side of the fish fillets. Add a glug of olive oil to the hot pan then add the coley, spice-side down. Cook for about 10 minutes, turning halfway when you've got a good bit of colour.
3 Check your rice - all the water should have been absorbed, so fluff it up with a fork and turn the heat off. Pop the lid back on so it stays warm.
4 Turn the heat under the fish up to high and throw in the greener slices from the top half of your spring onions. Add the remaining korma paste, coconut milk, coriander stalks and most of the chilli. Let it bubble for a couple of minutes until the fish is starting to flake apart. Taste your sauce and add a squeeze of lemon juice if needed.
5 Divide the rice between your plates then top each portion with a piece of coley. Pour the sauce over the top, then scatter over the reserved spring onions, chilli and coriander leaves. Serve with lemon wedges on the side for squeezing over.

HERRING LINGUINE

HERRING LINGUINE

I love herring. It's cheap, and cooking it like this makes it go further. It's not that popular in Britain, where most of it is exported or turned into fertiliser or fish feed. Cod and haddock usually feed on herring so, as their numbers decline, the herring population is rising. We need to eat further down the food chain!

Serves 4-6

- 500g linguine
- Olive oil
- 2 garlic cloves, finely sliced
- 1 red chilli, finely sliced
- 1 tbsp mini capers
- A small bunch of flat-leaf parsley, leaves chopped, stalks sliced
- 4 x 40g herring fillets, skin on, scaled, cut into strips
- A small handful of cherry tomatoes on the vine, quartered
- Juice of 1 lemon
- A knob of butter (optional)
- Extra-virgin olive oil

1 Cook the pasta in a pan of salted boiling water according to the packet instructions until al dente.
2 Meanwhile, put a large frying pan over a high heat and add a few glugs of olive oil. Once hot, add the garlic, chilli, capers and parsley stalks. Cook for a few minutes until starting to colour. Add the herring and cook for 2 minutes. They will start to break up but it's OK - this helps them stick to the pasta. Add the tomatoes and lemon juice.
3 Use tongs to transfer the cooked pasta straight into the frying pan, bringing a little of the cooking water with it. Add the butter, if using, and toss everything together in the pan. Taste and season, then add most of the parsley leaves and a glug of extra-virgin olive oil. Mix again - use tongs if you need to - then transfer to a large platter. Scatter over the remaining parsley leaves and whack it on the table so everyone can tuck in.

BARBECUED TROUT IN NEWSPAPER

Best-shellers

Fish is often passed over when it comes to barbecues, but oily fish (such as sardines and mackerel) are at their best when grilled. Cook them simply stuffed with herbs, or marinate for 30 minutes in a few different flavours first – this also works with white fish. Bash garlic with dried chilli, lemon juice and any herbs (and turmeric if you dare) and stir into yoghurt before smothering over the fish. Make North African chermoula by combining parsley, cumin and paprika; it's delicious with a preserved lemon and couscous salad. Rich fish like salmon works perfectly with sweet and sticky glazes, such as soy sauce, honey and sesame oil. Squid loves the barbecue, especially when tossed in fresh red chilli, coriander and lemon zest first. Or make a skewer with different bits of fish, a couple of bay leaves and a few vegetables.

BARBECUED TROUT IN NEWSPAPER

Serves 4

- 2 trout, gutted
- A bunch of coriander
- 2 lemongrass stalks, tough outer leaves removed, trimmed
- 6 kaffir lime leaves
- 4 garlic cloves
- A thumb-sized piece of ginger, sliced
- 1 red chilli (optional), sliced
- 4 limes, sliced, plus wedges to serve
- Olive oil

You will also need

- Newspaper
- Baking paper (optional)
- Unwaxed kitchen string

1 Preheat the barbecue so it's hot, or the coals turn white. Rinse the fish under cold water and pat dry with paper towel.
2 Twist off the stalks from the bunch of coriander and keep the leaves for the garnish. Put the lemongrass, kaffir lime leaves, garlic, ginger and coriander stalks in a large mortar with the chilli, if using, and use a pestle to bash them a bit to release the flavours.
3 For each trout, take a large double sheet of newspaper, line with baking paper, if using, and place a line of lime slices in the middle. Lay the fish on top and stuff the cavity with half the herby mixture, season with salt and drizzle with oil. Top with some lime slices and drizzle with more oil and salt.
4 Wrap up in newspaper and tie with string. Dunk both parcels in a bucket of water and leave to soak for no more than 5 minutes.
5 Barbecue the fish parcels, uncovered, for 30 minutes or until the flesh is firm. The newspaper will be black, but don't worry – the important thing is that the fish will be cooked to perfection.
6 Remove fish from the paper, drizzle with any juices, top with coriander leaves and serve with lime wedges.

SARDINES IN VINE LEAVES

Serves 2

- 6 vine leaves in brine (or cabbage or chard leaves)
- 6 sardines, gutted
- Olive oil
- Tomato salad, to serve

1 Preheat the oven to 200C/gas 6, or prepare a barbecue so that it's hot. Soak the vine leaves briefly in a bowl of cold water to rinse off the brine. Pat the leaves dry with paper towel. Place a sardine at one end of a leaf, season with salt and pepper and wrap up. Repeat with the remaining sardines until all are wrapped in a leaf.
2 Line a baking tray with foil and grease with a little olive oil. Place the fish parcels on the tray or hot barbecue, then brush with more olive oil. Bake in the oven or grill for 15 minutes and serve with a tomato salad or salsa.

MUSSELS WITH SMOKY BACON & CIDER

Mussels are the future. They're cheap, gorgeous, easy to farm and quick to cook. The other brilliant thing is that they live off plants filtered out of the water, so they actually clean the sea. They're one of the best things you can eat sustainably, so I want to help you fall back in love with them. I had my first mussel when I was about seven, and I remember it to this day. My kids love them - they're great fun to eat.

Serves 2 as a main, or 4 as a starter

- Olive oil
- 6 smoked streaky bacon rashers, sliced 1cm thick
- 1kg mussels, debearded and scrubbed clean
- 1 garlic clove, finely sliced
- 150ml good-quality cider
- 2 tbsp crème fraîche
- A small bunch of tarragon, leaves picked and chopped
- A small bunch of flat-leaf parsley, leaves picked and chopped

Toasts
- ½–1 loaf rustic bread, sliced 2cm thick
- 1 garlic clove, halved
- Extra-virgin olive oil

1 For the toasts, put your bread on a hot griddle, in the toaster or under a hot grill.
2 Meanwhile, add a glug of oil to a large pan over a high heat. Once hot, add the bacon and cook, stirring, until golden. Remove the bacon, leaving the fat. Check your mussels: if any are open, give them a tap; if they don't close they are bad, so bin them. Add the mussels to the pan with the garlic, cider and more olive oil. Cover with a lid. Steam for 3–4 minutes or until the mussels open.
3 Meanwhile, rub your toasts with the cut side of a garlic clove and drizzle lightly with extra-virgin olive oil.
4 Transfer the mussels to a platter, leaving the juices in the pan. If any are still closed, chuck them away. Lay your toasts around the platter.
5 Stir the crème fraîche into the pan. Let it come to the boil and bubble for a few minutes. Add most of the herbs and a little bacon. Taste and season with pepper. Jiggle the pan, then pour the sauce over your mussels. Scatter over the remaining herbs and bacon to serve.

MUSSEL SOUP

MUSSEL SOUP

Serves 4
- 1 large onion, sliced
- 2 tbsp chopped parsley
- 3 garlic cloves, chopped
- 100ml white wine, plus a splash extra
- 200g chopped tinned tomatoes
- 1kg mussels, cleaned
- Juice of ½ lemon
- Croutons

1 Fry the onion and parsley in a pan for 5 minutes until soft. Add the garlic and cook until starting to colour. Add the wine and cook for 7 minutes till reduced by half. Add the tomatoes and 200ml water, season and cook for 10 minutes.
2 Meanwhile, place the mussels and the extra splash of wine in a large pan over a medium-high heat. Cover and cook for 5 minutes, until they're all open. Allow to cool then take mussels out of their shells and stir into the soup. Add the lemon juice and serve with croutons.

MUSSELS & GUINNESS

Not pictured
Serves 2
- A knob of butter
- 2 garlic cloves, chopped
- 1 shallot, chopped
- 2 smoked bacon rashers, chopped
- A small bunch of thyme, leaves picked
- A small bunch of parsley, leaves picked
- 1 bay leaf
- 1 kg mussels, debearded, scrubbed
- 250ml Guinness
- 50ml double cream

1 Melt the butter in a pan. Add the garlic, shallot and bacon and cook gently for 4–5 minutes till soft. Add half the thyme and parsley, and the bay leaf. Season. Add the mussels and Guinness. Bring to the boil then cover and simmer for 3–5 minutes, till the mussels open.
2 Bin any unopened mussels. Stir in the cream and remaining herbs. Adjust the seasoning and serve with crusty bread.

SQUID STEW

SQUID STEW

Serves 2-3

- 2 tbsp olive oil
- 1 small red onion, finely chopped
- 2 garlic cloves, finely chopped
- 1 carrot, finely chopped
- 1 small fennel bulb, sliced
- 1 tsp fennel seeds
- 600g squid, cleaned and cut into rings
- A large glass of dry white wine
- 250g cherry tomatoes
- A small bunch of basil, leaves picked and torn

1 Heat the oil in a large frying pan over a gentle heat. Add the onion and cook until translucent. Add the garlic, carrot, fennel and fennel seeds and cook for a couple more minutes.
2 Turn the heat up and when the pan is nice and hot, add the squid and cook for several minutes until the squid turns opaque. Add the wine, turn down the heat and add the tomatoes. Simmer for about 15 minutes or until the squid is tender and the tomatoes have collapsed. Taste and season with salt and pepper, then add the torn basil leaves. Serve with spaghetti, rice or crusty bread.

BBQ SARDINES WITH GAZPACHO SHOTS

Gazpacho is a bit of a summer classic. For something a little different, serve it in shot glasses with crisp barbecued sardines and some lovely soft bread.

Serves 4

- 2 tbsp fennel seeds
- 1 tsp chilli flakes
- 1 tbsp flour
- 8 whole sardines, scaled and gutted
- Olive oil
- ½ bunch of lemon thyme
- 1 lemon, sliced
- A loaf of soft bread

Gazpacho
- A hunk of stale bread (about 100g)
- 2 tbsp red wine vinegar
- 1 cucumber, peeled, seeds scraped, roughly chopped
- 2 red peppers, deseeded, roughly chopped
- 1 garlic clove
- 6 ripe tomatoes, deseeded, roughly chopped
- Olive oil
- Mixed cress, to serve
- 2 spring onions, finely sliced on the diagonal

1 Preheat your grill to high or get your barbecue fired up so it's ready for later.
2 To make the gazpacho, tear up the stale bread and soak in the red wine vinegar for about 2 minutes. Add the soaked bread to a food processor with the cucumber, peppers, garlic clove and tomatoes and blitz until smooth. With the processor still running, add a good glug of oil. Have a taste and season with salt and pepper. If the gazpacho is a little too thick, add a few tablespoons of cold water and blitz again. Pop the soup in the fridge to chill while you cook the sardines.
3 In a pestle and mortar, bash the fennel seeds and most of the chilli flakes to a fine powder. Add the flour and a pinch of salt and pepper and mix in. Drizzle the sardines with a little oil then dip them in the spicy flour until evenly coated. Stuff a few sprigs of lemon thyme inside each fish, then line them up head to tail with slices of lemon in between. Thread 3 long metal skewers through all of the fish, making sure you spear the lemons too – this will make life easier when you turn them. Cook under the hot grill or on the barbecue for 4-5 minutes each side, or until cooked through with lovely spots of charred skin.
4 Pour the gazpacho into shot glasses and top each one with a little of the cress and spring onions. Serve with soft bread and crispy sardines, and enjoy sipping the little mouthfuls of spicy deliciousness.

BBQ SARDINES WITH GAZPACHO SHOTS

LANGOUSTINES WITH LEMON & PEPPER BUTTER

WHITING, LEEK & CAULIFLOWER GRATIN

CUTTLEFISH, SPINACH & POTATO

LANGOUSTINES WITH LEMON & PEPPER BUTTER

Frozen langoustines are usually sold pre-cooked, so you will probably need only defrost them before adding the topping. Cooking them in the wine won't be necessary.

Serves 4-6 as a starter

- 1kg langoustines, about 18, fresh if available
- 400ml white wine or water
- 50g fresh breadcrumbs
- Olive oil, to drizzle
- 2 lemons, halved
- Grated zest of 1 lemon, to serve

Lemon & pepper butter

- 100g butter, softened
- 2 tsp coarse black pepper
- Grated zest of 1 lemon

1 If your langoustines are frozen, defrost them completely.
2 For the lemon and pepper butter, combine all the ingredients and a pinch of salt in bowl. Set aside.
3 Heat a grill to a high heat. Meanwhile, combine the languoustines and wine, if using, in a pan. Bring to the boil, cover, then lower the heat and simmer for 5 minutes. Remove and cool slightly. Place your langoustines, belly-side down, on a chopping board and cut in half lengthways, discarding the black vein in the tail. Transfer, flesh-side up, to a baking tray, top with the lemon butter, sprinkle over the breadcrumbs, drizzle with oil, and add the lemon halves to the tray. Grill for 5-10 minutes, until golden - keep an eye on them . Serve the langoustines sprinkled with lemon zest, with the grilled lemon.

WHITING, LEEK & CAULIFLOWER GRATIN

Serves 2

- 220g whiting fillets, cut into pieces
- Olive oil
- 25g butter
- 50g flour
- 300ml milk
- 175g grated cheddar
- 25g parmesan, grated
- 100g cauliflower florets, parboiled
- 1 leek, thickly sliced and parboiled
- A handful of breadcrumbs

1 Preheat the oven to 180C/gas 4 and season the fish. Add a glug of olive oil to a pan over a high heat and fry the fish for 1-2 minutes, until partially cooked. Remove from the heat and set aside.
2 In a separate pan, melt the butter and add the flour. Cook, stirring, over a low heat for 4-5 minutes. Slowly pour in the milk, stirring constantly until you have a thick, smooth sauce. Season well and add half of each of the cheeses. Stir in the vegetables, followed by the fish, and mix well. Transfer to a baking dish, sprinkle with the remaining cheese and the breadcrumbs and drizzle with oil. Bake in the oven for 20 minutes, or till golden on top.

CUTTLEFISH, SPINACH & POTATO

Serves 4

- Olive oil
- 1 onion, sliced
- 2 garlic cloves, sliced
- ½ tbsp each dried oregano and mint 1 tbsp olive oil
- 750g cuttlefish, cleaned and chopped
- 1 x 400g tin chopped tomatoes
- 2 tbsp chopped parsley leaves
- 175ml white wine
- 450g spinach
- 750g potatoes, chopped and boiled

1 Heat a glug of olive oil in a large frying pan. Add the onion, garlic and herbs and cook over a medium heat until soft. Add the cuttlefish and cook, stirring, for 5 minutes until opaque. Stir in the tomatoes, parsley and white wine and add enough water to cover. Season and leave to simmer for 50 minutes.
2 Add the spinach and cook until wilted. Add the boiled potatoes and serve hot.

LEMON SOLE WITH CHIPOTLE & ANCHO CHILLI RECADO

LEMON SOLE WITH CHIPOTLE & ANCHO CHILLI RECADO

Serves 4

- 4 lemon sole or dab fillets, skin on
- Lime wedges, to serve

Chipotle & ancho chilli recado

- 4 garlic cloves, unpeeled
- 2 dried chipotle chillies
- 2 dried ancho chillies
- 1½ tbsp dried oregano
- Juice of ½ lime

Avocado & cherry tomato salad

- 14 cherry tomatoes, halved
- 1 lebanese cucumber, sliced
- 3 spring onions, including tops, sliced
- 1 avocado, roughly chopped
- 3 tbsp olive oil
- Juice of 1 lime

1 Preheat the oven to 180C/gas 4. To make the recado, place the garlic in a small roasting tin and roast for 15–20 minutes or until soft. Transfer to a plate, let cool then remove the skins.
2 Place the chipotle and ancho chillies in a small bowl of boiling water and soak for 15 minutes. Drain in a colander set over a bowl, reserving the liquid.
3 Place the chillies, garlic, oregano and a pinch of salt in a food processor and blend to a paste. Add the lime juice and 4 tablespoons of reserved liquid and blitz. Transfer to a nonreactive bowl.
4 Place the fish in the marinade, cover with clingfilm and chill for 30 minutes.
5 Preheat a barbecue or cast-iron griddle pan to a medium heat. Remove the fish from the fridge and cook, turning once, for about 3 minutes each side, occasionally brushing on some more marinade during cooking.
6 For the salad, combine all ingredients in a bowl and season. Divide the fish among plates and serve with the avocado salad and lime wedges.

CRAB CAKES & HOT BLACKENED SALSA

Serves 6

- 500g potatoes, large ones halved
- 500g mixed brown and white crab meat (2:1 brown to white)
- Zest of 1 lemon, plus wedges to serve
- A few flat-leaf parsley sprigs
- ½ red chilli

CRAB CAKES & HOT BLACKENED SALSA

- 3 spring onions
- Olive oil

Salsa

- Olive oil
- 1 red pepper, quartered, deseeded
- 10 cherry tomatoes on the vine
- 1 red chilli, halved lengthways, deseeded
- 1 spring onion
- 3 tbsp extra-virgin olive oil
- Juice of ½ lemon
- A few basil sprigs, leaves picked

1 Add the potatoes to a large pan of salted boiling water and cook for 15–20 minutes or until tender.
2 Drain the potatoes, steam dry, then return to the pan. Season, then add the crab meat and mash with a potato masher. Finely grate the lemon zest onto a board, add the parsley, chilli and spring onions and chop it all together, mixing as you go, until fine. Scrape this into the pan of crab and mash again to combine. Divide into 12 portions and shape each one into a patty. Transfer to a large plate, cover with clingfilm and place in the fridge for at least 4 hours, or overnight, to firm up.
3 Meanwhile for the salsa, add a splash of olive oil to a large pan over a high heat. Blacken the pepper, tomatoes and chilli then cool and set aside.
4 When ready to cook, add a splash of oil to a large pan over a high heat. Add 6 patties and cook for about 5 minutes, turning halfway, or until golden, crisp and cooked through, then repeat with the second batch.
5 Meanwhile, chop the blackened veg and spring onion. Have a taste, then season and add the extra-virgin olive oil and lemon juice. Add the basil and chop until you're happy with the consistency.
6 To serve, lay the crab cakes out on a platter and top with the salsa. Serve with a simple rocket salad and lemon wedges for squeezing over.

CRISPY CHORIZO & SQUID SALAD

CRISPY CHORIZO & SQUID SALAD

This Spanish-style salad is great with a glass of chilled sherry or sweet wine. It's reminiscent of a balmy summer's evening in Spain, so close your eyes and pretend you're there.

Serves 4 as a starter

• 1 red onion, finely sliced
• Sherry vinegar
• 100g raw chorizo, finely sliced
• 4 squid, cleaned, tentacles reserved, finely sliced
• Olive oil
• ½ bunch of flat-leaf parsley, leaves picked

1 Pile up the sliced red onion on a platter, add a splash of sherry vinegar and gently toss so it starts to pickle slightly. Set aside.
2 Meanwhile, fry the chorizo in a pan over a medium heat for 3-4 minutes, or until it's crispy and all the fat has rendered out. Add a good splash of sherry vinegar and toss it all around, then set aside.
3 Meanwhile, season the squid tubes and tentacles, then fry in a pan with a splash of olive oil over a high heat for 2-3 minutes, until golden.
4 Quickly toss the parsley leaves with the red onion. Scatter over the chorizo, then top with the squid and eat straight away.

SUMMER SEAFOOD SALAD

You can buy pre-cooked seafood salad but it's nice to do your own. I like clams, cockles and mussels, but use what you can get. The spicy tomato sauce is inspired by a bloody mary - but here we've skipped vodka.

Serves 6

• 2kg mixture of clams, cockles and mussels
• 1 garlic clove
• Extra-virgin olive oil
• A splash of white wine

SUMMER SEAFOOD SALAD

• 4 squid, cleaned, tentacles reserved, finely sliced
• Juice of ½ lemon
• ½ bunch of flat-leaf parsley, leaves picked and chopped
• A few leafy fennel tops (optional)
• Brown bread and butter, to serve

Virgin mary dressing

• 6 tomatoes, halved
• 2 garlic cloves
• 2 tbsp white wine vinegar
• 2 tbsp tomato ketchup
• 2 tsp jarred grated horseradish
• 1 red chilli, deseeded
• Juice of 1 lemon
• A splash of Tabasco

1 Pick through the shellfish and tap any that are open. If any don't close, throw those ones away.
2 Add the garlic, a drizzle of olive oil, the white wine and the shellfish to a large frying pan. Pop the lid on, shake gently, and cook over a medium-high heat for 3-4 minutes, or until the shellfish have opened. Add all the squid, stir, then put the lid back on the pan and remove from the heat to let the squid cook through in the residual heat for about 5 minutes.
3 Meanwhile for the sauce, whizz all the ingredients together in a blender until smooth. Tip the pan of shellfish into a colander set over a bowl to catch the drained liquid. Add the cooking liquid to the blender, whizz again and taste. Adjust the seasoning and add some more Tabasco, if you like.
4 Pick all the shellfish into a bowl, and discard the shells. Throw away any shellfish that are still closed. Add the squid and dress the lot with lemon juice and a drizzle of olive oil.
5 Pour the sauce through a sieve onto a lovely dish, then top with the dressed seafood. Scatter over the chopped parsley and fennel tops, if using, and serve the seafood salad with sliced brown bread and butter.

SCALLOPS & CREME FRAICHE EN CROUTE

BRILL WITH SORREL SAUCE

SCALLOPS & CREME FRAICHE EN CROUTE

These little pies make a fun, retro dinner-party starter.

Serves 6 as a starter

- A knob of butter, plus a little extra for greasing
- 300g puff pastry
- 1 egg, beaten
- 12 small scallops
- A good splash of cider
- 2 tbsp crème fraîche
- 2 tbsp (total) chopped parsley, chervil and chives

1 Preheat the oven to 200C/gas 6. Grease a baking tray with butter. Roll out the pastry to about 5mm thick and cut into six 8cm rounds. Place on the baking tray and, with a sharp knife, score a circle on each, about 1cm from the edge, being careful not to cut all the way through the pastry. Prick the centres with a fork then brush the edges only with the beaten egg, being careful not to get any into the scored lines, otherwise the pastry won't rise properly. Place the rounds in the oven and cook for 5 minutes, or until golden and risen. Take out of the oven and gently remove the top layers from the centre of each pastry round by placing a sharp knife under the scored border and lifting gently.

2 Melt the butter in a pan over a high heat. Season each scallop and place in the hot pan, cooking on each side for 1-2 minutes or until golden. Add the cider and cook for 1 minute before transferring the scallops to a warm plate. Add the crème fraîche and herbs to the pan, stir, and season well. Place a scallop in each pastry case, spoon over the sauce and top with a pastry lid.

BRILL WITH SORREL SAUCE

Brill is a flat fish similar to turbot but a bit cheaper, and, because it's also a little smaller, it can be easier to handle. Cooking brill simply like this lets its flavour shine through.

Serves 4-6

- 1 brill (about 1.3kg), cleaned
- 1 lemon, sliced
- 2 shallots, finely chopped
- Olive oil
- 550ml cider
- 2 tbsp crème fraîche
- 2 bunches of sorrel, sliced

1 Preheat the oven to 220C/gas 7. Place the brill in a large roasting dish and stuff the cavity with the lemon slices and a quarter of the shallots. Season generously, drizzle with a little olive oil and bake for 40 minutes, or

until cooked through but not dry. After 10 minutes of cooking, pour over 300ml cider. Warm a serving platter in the oven. Once the fish is only just cooked, remove from the pan and loosely cover with tin foil - remember, it will keep cooking - while you make the sauce.
2 Place the roasting dish over a medium heat and sauté the remaining shallots in the fish juices with a little oil until soft. Pour in the remaining cider. Bring to the boil, then simmer for 2 minutes to reduce. Stir in the crème fraîche and sorrel. Season to taste, then serve immediately with the brill.

BROWN SHRIMPS ON TOAST

This is quick and simple to make, so it's perfect as a starter or a lazy weekend brunch.

Serves 4 as a starter or 2 as a main

- A knob of butter
- 200g brown shrimps
- 100ml cider
- Toast, to serve

1 Melt the butter in a frying pan over a medium heat and add the shrimps. Pour in the cider and bring to the boil, then turn down the heat and simmer for 3 minutes until the cider has reduced. Season with pepper and serve on toast.

EASY
SUPPER

I.O.SHEN
MASTERGRADE
The Choice of Professionals
at affordable prices
"I truly believe that I.O.Shen knives are the strongest, sharpest and best knives I have ever used."
Mike Robinson, Countrywise Kitchen & The Pot Kiln
Multi award winning Japanese steel knives
UK – www.ioshen.co.uk
01869 357700
The UK's fastest growing knife brand with prices starting from £44.95
Available at Jamie Oliver Recipease and good cook shops
Australia – www.ioshen.com.au
1300 650 656

POULTRY

PETITE BLANQUETTE DE POULET A L'ESTRAGON

Tarragon chicken
Recipe from Boundary
Serves 4-6

- 3 tbsp olive oil
- 1 x 1.4kg chicken, cut into 8 pieces
- 1 large carrot, roughly chopped
- 1 celery stalk, roughly chopped
- 1 large onion, finely chopped
- 150g button mushrooms, quartered
- 50ml white wine
- 1 bunch of thyme, tied with string
- 5 bay leaves
- 500ml chicken stock
- 40g flour
- 40g butter, softened
- Juice of 1 lemon
- 220ml whipping cream
- 2 egg yolks, beaten
- 2 tbsp chopped tarragon

1 Heat 2 tablespoons of the olive oil in a large pan over a high heat. Add the chicken, in batches if necessary, and cook until browned on all sides. Remove from the pan and set aside.
2 Wipe out the pan with kitchen paper then heat the remaining oil. Add the carrot, celery and onion and cook over a medium heat for 5 minutes, until the onion is soft. Add the mushrooms and cook for a further 5 minutes. Add the wine and simmer until reduced by half.
3 Return the chicken to the pan with the thyme, bay and stock. Simmer, covered, for 40-50 minutes or till the chicken is falling off the bone. Spoon the chicken and vegetables into a serving dish and keep warm. Strain the cooking liquid into a saucepan.
4 Whisk together the flour and butter, add to the cooking liquid, whisking continuously, and place over a medium heat. Bring to the boil then reduce the heat and simmer for 5 minutes. Add the lemon juice and season to taste.
5 Combine the cream and egg yolks in a jug and whisk into the sauce. Stir in the tarragon, pour the sauce over the chicken and serve.

COQ AU RIESLING

COQ AU RIESLING

Recipe from Lutyens
Using riesling instead of red wine (usually burgundy), makes this coq au vin typical of the Alsace region.
Serves 8-10

- 2 x 1.5-1.75kg chickens, each cut into 8 pieces
- 50g butter
- Olive oil
- 250g smoked streaky bacon, sliced
- 500g baby or pearl onions, larger ones halved
- 500g button mushrooms, cleaned, larger ones halved
- ½ bunch of thyme, leaves picked
- 250ml riesling
- 400ml chicken stock
- 100ml crème fraîche
- A large bunch of parsley

1 Rinse each piece of chicken in cold water and pat dry with kitchen towel. Season with sea salt and set aside.

2 Melt half the butter and a little oil in large pan. Add the chicken and cook, in batches if necessary, over a medium-high heat until golden on all sides. Remove from the pan and set aside. Add the bacon to the pan and cook until golden brown. Remove from the pan and set aside.
3 Wipe out the pan then add remaining butter. When it starts to foam, add the onion and mushrooms and cook over a medium heat till golden and softened.
4 Return the chicken and bacon to the pan with the thyme. Add the wine and stock. Bring to the boil. Cover, reduce to a simmer and cook for 30 minutes. Check the chicken is cooked through; if not, cook 15 minutes more. Once cooked, remove the chicken and set aside. Turn the heat up and reduce the sauce for about 10 minutes, or until thickened. Return the chicken to the pan, add the crème fraîche and parsley. Season to taste. Transfer to a nice dish and serve.

POMEGRANATE & CHICKEN STEW

POMEGRANATE & CHICKEN STEW

Serves 4-6

- 1-2 tbsp olive oil
- 1 chicken, jointed
- 1 tsp paprika
- 2 onions, sliced
- 4 garlic cloves, finely chopped
- 1 red chilli, finely sliced
- 2 tbsp finely chopped coriander, plus extra for the rice
- 300ml tomato passata
- 4 tbsp pomegranate molasses
- About 200ml pomegranate juice
- Boiled rice and pomegranate seeds

1 Heat the olive oil in a casserole over a medium heat. Season the chicken pieces with salt, pepper and paprika, then brown for 7–8 minutes. Remove the chicken to a plate and set aside.
2 Add another splash of oil to the pan and add the onions. Stir well, being sure to catch the sticky bits at the bottom of the pan. Cook over a low-medium heat for 15 minutes, till the onions are soft. Add the garlic, chilli and coriander for the last 5 minutes. Stir in the passata, molasses and pomegranate juice, season well, then bring to the boil.
3 Return the chicken and any juices to the pan, cover and lower the heat. Simmer for 30 minutes, until the chicken is cooked and the sauce has thickened (check often that it's not sticking). Toss the rice with the extra coriander, then place the chicken on top and scatter with pomegranate seeds.

POULET BASQUAISE

Basque-style chicken
Recipe from Boundary
Serves 4-6

- 1 tbsp flour
- 1½ tsp piment d'espelette (or paprika)
- 1 x 1.4kg chicken, cut into 8 pieces
- 3 tbsp olive oil
- 1 large white onion, sliced
- 2 garlic cloves, sliced
- 2 red peppers, thinly sliced
- 2 yellow peppers, thinly sliced
- 50ml white wine
- 900g tomatoes, skinned, chopped (or 2 x 400g tins chopped tomatoes)
- 750ml chicken stock
- ½ bunch of thyme, tied with string
- 5 bay leaves
- Juice of ½ lemon
- ½ bunch of parsley, chopped

1 Place the flour in a bowl, season generously then stir in the piment d'espelette. Dredge the chicken in the seasoned flour and set aside.
2 Heat 2 tablespoons of olive oil in a large stockpot and cook the chicken till golden all over. Remove and set aside.
3 Wipe out the pan, add the remaining oil and cook the onion over a medium heat for 3 minutes until softened. Add the garlic and peppers and cook for a further 5 minutes until softened. Add the wine and allow to reduce until almost dry, then stir in the tomatoes.
4 Return the chicken to the pan. Add the stock, thyme and bay leaves, cover with a lid and simmer for 45 minutes. Add the lemon juice and parsley then taste and adjust the seasoning with piment d'espelette and salt.

POULET BASQUAISE

CHILLI CHICKEN WINGS

CORIANDER & LEMON DRUMSTICKS

CHICKEN SALTIMBOCCA
Serves 2

- 2 chicken breasts, skin on
- 12 sage leaves
- 4 smoked streaky bacon rashers, halved
- Barbecued cherry tomatoes and lime wedges, to serve

1 Place 2 long layers of clingfilm on a board. Place the chicken breasts on top, skin-side up, a few inches apart. For each breast, gently separate part of the skin from the meat and insert 3 sage leaves. Turn the chicken over and place 3 sage leaves on the other side, then cover with 4 pieces of bacon.
2 Cover chicken with another 2 layers of clingfilm, then use a rolling pin to bash the meat to less than 1cm thick.
3 Remove the clingfilm. Season the skin side of the chicken with salt, and the bacon side with pepper. Barbecue or cook on a hot griddle pan, skin-side down, for 2 minutes, then turn and cook the bacon side for 2 minutes, or until the chicken is cooked through. Serve immediately with tomatoes or any vegetables you like, with lime wedges.

CHILLI CHICKEN WINGS
Serves 6

- 100ml Asian-style hot chilli sauce
- 2 tbsp honey
- 1 tbsp soy sauce
- 2 tsp sesame oil
- 18 chicken wings
- 30g toasted sesame seeds

1 Place the chilli sauce, honey, soy sauce and sesame oil in a large nonreactive mixing bowl. Mix well until the honey has dissolved.
2 Add the chicken wings, toss to coat and leave to marinate for 20 minutes. If you want to leave them for any longer, cover the bowl with clingfilm and refrigerate, removing from the fridge in time for the chicken to reach room temperature before cooking.
3 Cook the wings on a medium-hot barbecue or frying pan, turning and basting with the marinade, until dark, sticky and cooked through. Remove from the barbecue and scatter with the toasted sesame seeds before serving.

CORIANDER & LEMON DRUMSTICKS
Serves 4

- 1 large bunch of coriander
- 2 lemongrass stalks, tough outer leaves removed, trimmed
- 5cm piece of ginger, chopped
- Grated zest and juice of 2 lemons
- A large pinch of brown sugar
- About 100ml vegetable oil
- 8 chicken drumsticks

1 Blitz the coriander, lemongrass and ginger in a food processor until finely chopped. Transfer to a large nonreactive bowl and add the zest, juice, sugar and a large pinch of salt. Stir in the oil. Taste, and add more sugar or lemon if desired. Reserve 2 tablespoons of the marinade in a small bowl. Cut a few slashes in the drumsticks, then add to the large bowl, coat in the marinade and leave to marinate. If leaving for longer than 20 minutes, cover the bowl with clingfilm and refrigerate, then bring to room temperature before cooking.
2 When you're ready to cook, remove the chicken from the marinade and cook on a hot barbecue or fryin pan, turning regularly and basting, for 10–12 minutes or until done. Don't worry if they look burnt; the marinade may blacken. Serve the cooked drumsticks with a drizzle of the reserved marinade.

LEVI ROOTS-STYLEE JERK CHICKEN & JALAPENO BREADS

LEVI ROOTS-STYLEE JERK CHICKEN & JALAPENO BREADS

Serves 4

- 1 tbsp black peppercorns
- 1 tbsp allspice berries
- 1 tbsp dried chilli flakes
- ½ tbsp muscovado sugar
- 2 tbsp runny honey
- A few flat-leaf parsley sprigs
- A few coriander sprigs
- 2 scotch bonnet chillies
- 1 garlic clove
- 3cm piece of ginger
- 2 spring onions, finely sliced
- Olive oil
- 4 chicken thighs and 4 drumsticks
- Beer, for drizzling (optional)
- 1 lime

Jalapeno breads
- 250g self-raising flour, plus extra
- 250g yoghurt
- ½ tsp baking powder
- 1 jalapeno chilli, finely sliced

1 Using a pestle and mortar, pound the black peppercorns, allspice berries and chilli flakes until fine, then mix in the sugar and honey. Finely chop the herbs, chillies, garlic and ginger, add to the spice mixture and bash it all up some more. Add the green parts of the spring onions and a good drizzle of oil and mix well. Pour the marinade over the chicken and massage it into the skin and all over - wear rubber gloves if you want, as those chillies are hot! Marinate in the fridge for at least 1-2 hours, but preferably overnight.
2 Place the chicken, skin-side down, on the barbecue over a medium heat. Cook for 40-50 minutes, turning often, or until golden and the juices run clear. You could also cook it in a tray in a 200C/ gas 6 oven for 25-30 minutes, turning occasionally, and finish on the barbecue for 5 minutes to get lovely and charred.
3 Meanwhile for the breads, mix together the flour, yoghurt, baking powder and a good pinch of salt. When it starts coming together, flour your hands and knead the dough on a lightly floured surface. Divide the dough into 4 pieces then roll out into circles about 2mm thick. Scatter over the jalapeno and a pinch of salt and press into the dough. Quickly scrub off any burnt jerk rub from half your barbecue bars, then use kitchen paper to rub the bars with olive oil. Add the breads and cook for 2-3 minutes, turning once, until golden brown on both sides. When the chicken is ready, squeeze over a little lime juice, then take off the grill and serve with the jalapeno breads.

SATAY CHICKEN STIR-FRY

Serves 2

- Groundnut oil
- 1 onion, cut in thin wedges
- 2 garlic cloves, chopped
- 1 red chilli, deseeded and sliced
- A thumb-sized piece of ginger, grated
- 1 lemongrass stalk, halved
- 2 chicken breasts, sliced
- 50g crunchy peanut butter
- 2 tbsp fish sauce
- 2 tbsp soy sauce
- 1 tbsp sugar
- 400ml coconut milk
- 200g udon noodles, cooked
- A handful of bean sprouts
- Lime wedges and sliced spring onions, to serve

1 Heat some groundnut oil in a wok. Fry the onion, garlic, red chilli, ginger and lemongrass until golden. Add the chicken and fry for a few minutes. Stir in the peanut butter, fish sauce, soy, sugar and coconut milk. Boil, then simmer for 5-10 minutes. When the chicken is cooked and hot, stir through the noodles and bean sprouts. Serve with lime wedges and spring onions.

STICKY SESAME SPATCHCOCKED BIRDS

A toast to roasts

Roast chicken is the ultimate easy dinner and can be done in many different ways. For a piri-piri-style roast, rub the skin with smoked paprika, dried oregano, lemon juice and olive oil. In Italy, they often pot-roast their birds with whole milk, lemon rind and sage for a rich sauce. Or try sitting your chicken on a bed of potatoes, apples and thyme and pouring over cider halfway through cooking. You could also rub a chicken with chilli, cumin and coriander seeds, place it on a bed of couscous and vegetables, and add a dash of water to the dish before covering and cooking. Spatchcocking is a good way to get lots of crisp skin. Try stuffing the skin with a mix of chopped sage leaves, lemon zest and mascarpone, or boil a few garlic cloves and smash them with parsley, fennel seeds and olive oil then stuff the paste between the meat and the skin.

EASY CLASSIC

SUMMER ROAST CHICKEN

STICKY SESAME SPATCHCOCKED BIRDS

Ask your butcher to spatchcock the quail for you – this means removing the backbone and breaking the chest bone so the bird can be laid out flat. It's perfect for barbecuing or grilling, as you'll get a bigger surface area and the meat will cook more evenly.
Serves 4
- 4 whole quails (about 750g each), spatchcocked
- 2 tbsp tahini
- 2 tbsp runny honey, plus extra
- 2 tbsp sesame seeds

Marinade
- 2 garlic cloves, finely sliced
- 5cm piece of ginger, finely grated
- Juice of 3 limes
- 2 tbsp soy sauce, plus extra

1 Combine the marinade ingredients. Pour three-quarters into a large, sealable sandwich bag and put the rest in the fridge for later. Put the quails in the bag, jiggle to coat, then put in the fridge to marinate for at least 4 hours.
2 When you're ready to cook, push 2 parallel skewers through 2 quails – under the wings and under and through the legs. This will make them easier to move around and ensure they don't get too close to the coals.
3 Cook the quails over a medium-hot part of the barbecue or in your griddle pan for 12–15 minutes, or until golden brown, turning every few minutes. Meanwhile, mix the reserved marinade with the tahini and honey. When the birds are cooked through, start basting them with this mixture to build up layers of flavour and create a sweet, sticky crust. After a couple of minutes, sprinkle over the sesame seeds and let them toast for a couple of minutes.
4 To serve, mix a swirl each of extra honey and soy through the reserved marinade and pour over the quail.

SUMMER ROAST CHICKEN

Serves 4–6
- 1 head of garlic
- 25g basil, leaves only, torn
- 50g butter, softened
- 1 chicken
- 1 carrot, chopped
- 1 onion, cut into wedges
- 1 celery stalk, chopped
- 2 lemons, 1 sliced, 1 halved
- Olive oil

1 Preheat the oven to 180C/gas 4. Crush 2 garlic cloves. Mix with basil and butter, season and spread over chicken. Squash half the remaining garlic and put in the bird's cavity. Put the rest in an oven tray with the veg. Place the sliced lemon on top. Squeeze the halved lemon over the bird then place in the cavity.
2 Drizzle the chicken with olive oil and place on the veg. Roast in the oven for 1 hour, or until the juices run clear.

DUCK WITH PUMPKIN SEED RECADO & PALM HEART SALAD

DUCK WITH PUMPKIN SEED RECADO & PALM HEART SALAD

Serves 4

- 4 duck breasts, skin slashed 3 or 4 times

Pumpkin seed recado

- 2 garlic cloves, unpeeled
- 2 plum tomatoes, quartered
- 1 white onion, cut into 8 wedges
- 2 fresh jalapeno chillies, halved and deseeded
- 90g pumpkin seeds
- 1 tbsp dried oregano
- 1 tsp cumin seeds
- 1 tbsp dried mint
- 3 tbsp coriander leaves, roughly chopped
- Juice of 1 lime
- 50ml olive oil

Palm heart & avocado salad

- 1 x 410g tin palm hearts, drained and roughly chopped
- 2 avocados, peeled, stoned, sliced
- Seeds from 1 pomegranate
- 2 tbsp olive oil
- Juice of 1 lime

ORIENTAL CHICKEN

1 Preheat the oven to 200C/gas 6. To make the recado, place the garlic, tomatoes, onion and jalapenos in a roasting tin and roast in the oven for 30 minutes, covering with foil halfway through, until all ingredients are soft but not blackened. Transfer to a plate and leave to cool.

2 Meanwhile, heat a large pan over a low heat. Generously sprinkle the duck skins with sea salt then place in the pan and cook for 12–15 minutes or until some fat is released. Drain the duck on kitchen paper and set aside. Discard the fat, or save it to use for roast potatoes another time.

3 Heat a frying pan over a medium heat. Add the pumpkin seeds and toast for 5 minutes, or until beginning to char. Transfer to a food processor with a pinch of ground black pepper and 1 tablespoon of salt. Add the cooled jalapeno mixture and all the remaining recado ingredients and blend until you have a thick paste.

4 Transfer the recado to a large nonreactive bowl and add the duck

breasts. Mix to coat well then cover with clingfilm and place in the fridge to marinate for 3–4 hours, or overnight.

5 Remove the duck from the fridge and bring to room temperature. Preheat a barbecue or cast-iron griddle pan to medium heat. Cook the duck, turning once, for about 10 minutes each side, occasionally brushing on more of the marinade during cooking.

6 For the palm heart salad, combine the palm hearts, avocado and pomegranate seeds in a large serving dish. Add the olive oil and lime juice and season with salt and black pepper. Slice the cooked duck breasts, place on top of the salad and serve immediately.

....

ORIENTAL CHICKEN

Serves 4

- 50ml sesame oil
- 150ml rice wine vinegar
- 4 tsp crushed sichuan peppercorns
- 2 fresh red chillies, sliced
- 5 tbsp dark soy sauce
- 2 tbsp honey
- 8 chicken thighs, skin slashed
- Coriander sprigs, sliced chillies and sliced spring onions, to serve

1 Combine the sesame oil, vinegar, peppercorns, chillies, 2 tablespoons of soy sauce and 1 tablespoon of honey in a large nonreactive bowl. Add the chicken to the bowl, toss to coat, then leave to marinate for 20 minutes. (Refrigerate the chicken, covered, if you wish to marinate it for any longer, but return it to room temperature before cooking.)

2 Mix the remaining soy sauce and honey together in a bowl. Remove the chicken from the marinade and cook on a medium-hot barbecue, basting with the soy mix until dark, sticky and cooked through. Serve with coriander, extra chillies and spring onions.

BRAISED GUINEA FOWLS, ROOT VEG & LENTILS

BRAISED GUINEA FOWLS, ROOT VEG & LENTILS

Serves 8
- 2 guinea fowls
- 1 tbsp butter
- 4 shallots, halved
- 2 garlic cloves, roughly chopped
- 3 tbsp chopped parsley
- 100g sultanas
- A generous splash of calvados
- 750ml cider
- 5 bay leaves
- 1 celery heart, sliced into 8 segments
- 200g baby carrots
- 400g each of swede, parsnip and turnips, cut into large chunks
- 180g baby fennel

Lentils
- 250g lentils
- 1 garlic clove
- 1 bay leaf
- 400g brussels sprout tops, blanched
- Olive oil

1 Season the guinea fowls well. Melt the butter in a large ovenproof pan over a medium heat and brown the guinea fowls, turning as necessary. Add the shallots, garlic, parsley and sultanas and cook until softened a little. Add the calvados, cider and bay leaves then cover and cook over a low heat for 90 minutes. After 30 minutes, add all the vegetables and season to taste. Check regularly to make sure it hasn't become too dry, and add a little more cider or water if necessary.
2 Meanwhile, place the lentils, garlic and bay in a saucepan and cover with cold water. Bring to the boil then simmer for about 30 minutes, or until the lentils are soft and cooked. Remove from the heat, add a good pinch of salt and leave to stand for 5 minutes. Stir in the brussels sprout tops then drain. Finish with a splash of olive oil. Spoon onto a platter, top with the guinea fowls and serve with the vegetables in cider.

QUAIL WITH GARLIC RECADO

Serves 6
- 6 quails, butterflied
- Warm tortillas and lime wedges, to serve

Spicy garlic recado
- 1 whole garlic head, unpeeled
- 3 dried guajillo chillies or other dried Mexican chillies
- 1 tbsp dried oregano
- 1 tbsp ground cumin
- 1 tbsp coriander seeds
- 1 tbsp sea salt
- Juice of 2 oranges

1 Preheat the oven to 200C/gas 6. For the recado, place the garlic in a small roasting dish and roast for 30 minutes or until the cloves are soft. Transfer to a plate and allow to cool, then peel.
2 Place the chillies in a bowl and pour over a cupful of boiling water. Leave the chillies to soak for 15 minutes then drain in a colander set over a bowl, reserving the liquid.
3 Place the roasted garlic flesh, chillies, oregano, cumin, coriander seeds, salt and a pinch of freshly ground black pepper in a food processor and blend to a thick paste. Add the orange juice and about 4 tablespoons of the reserved chilli liquid and briefly pulse to combine. Transfer the recado mixture to a large nonreactive bowl.
4 Place the quails in the recado, turning to coat, then cover with clingfilm and place in the fridge to marinate for 3-4 hours, or overnight.
5 When ready to cook, remove the quails from the fridge and bring to room temperature. Preheat a barbecue or cast-iron griddle pan to a medium heat. Cook the quails, turning once, for 12-15 minutes on each side, or until cooked through. Occasionally brush on more of the recado during cooking.
6 Divide the quails among serving plates and serve with the warm tortillas, lime wedges to squeeze over, and Mexican beers, if you like.

QUAIL WITH GARLIC RECADO

Our independent auditor James has had a fantastic year, ticking over 6000 boxes.

James – this magnificent Cottage Pie is for you.

Quality Standard beef is all thanks to some very pernickety people. To guarantee succulence and tenderness, it takes an array of independent auditors and box tickers. They are responsible for scrutinizing every aspect of the meat's journey, from farm to fork. Look out for the label.

For tasty beef recipes go to simplybeef.co.uk

QUALITY STANDARD beef English

Tough standards. Tender results.

CRUSTED LAMB RACK WITH RHUBARB

CRUSTED LAMB RACK WITH RHUBARB

This almond- and herb-coated lamb gives a twist to your Sunday roast.

Serves 6

- 750g rhubarb, trimmed and sliced into 5cm pieces
- 6 tbsp honey
- Extra-virgin olive oil
- 75g whole or flaked almonds
- Large bunch of mixed herbs, such as parsley, mint and chives, leaves picked
- A handful of breadcrumbs
- 2 x 6-bone racks of lamb
- 2 tbsp dijon mustard

1 Preheat oven to 200C/gas 6. Place the rhubarb in a roasting tray. Drizzle with honey and a good glug of oil, mix well to coat, then spread evenly over the pan.
2 Blitz the almonds in a food processor with the herbs, then transfer to a bowl. Stir in the breadcrumbs and season with salt and ground black pepper.

3 Using a sharp knife, score the fat on the lamb, rub in the mustard, then pat on the breadcrumb mix. Place the lamb on the rhubarb, drizzle with oil and cook for 25–35 minutes for medium, or 5–10 more minutes for well done. Rest for 5–10 minutes, then carve into cutlets and serve with the rhubarb.

ROAST LAMB PIE

Serves 12

- 75g butter, plus 50g, melted, to grease
- 3 tbsp olive oil
- 2 celery stalks, sliced
- 2 leeks, thinly sliced
- 2 onions, thinly sliced
- 3 garlic cloves, finely chopped
- 1kg roast lamb, chopped
- 60g currants or raisins
- 300g feta, crumbled
- 500g potatoes, diced and parboiled
- 180g long grain rice, parboiled
- ½ tbsp ground cinnamon
- 1 tbsp dried mint
- 1 tbsp dried oregano
- ½ bunch of flat-leaf parsley, including stalks, finely chopped
- 2 x 270g packets filo pastry
- 3 eggs, hardboiled and quartered
- 1 tbsp za'atar (see note)

1 Heat the butter and oil in a frying pan and sauté the celery, leeks, onions and garlic for 5-7 minutes, until softened. Add the roast lamb and cook, stirring occasionally, for 2–3 minutes. Transfer to a bowl and set aside to cool.
2 Preheat the oven to 180C/gas 4. Lightly grease a shallow 40cm x 30cm roasting dish. When the lamb mixture has cooled, add the currants, feta, potato, rice, cinnamon, mint, oregano and parsley and mix well. Set aside.
3 Lay 1 sheet of filo in the roasting dish and brush with melted butter. Repeat until you have used all of 1 packet.
4 Spread the lamb filling over the filo pastry, then top with the hardboiled egg quarters, in evenly spaced rows.
5 Place 1 sheet of filo from the second packet of pastry on top of the filling, brush with melted butter and continue layering until you've used all the pastry.
6 Sprinkle over the za'atar and cut the lamb pie into 12 squares, making sure each square contains some egg. Drizzle over a little cold water and bake in the oven for 1 hour, or until the top is golden and the pastry and filling cooked through. Cool slightly before serving.
Note Za'atar is a Middle Eastern herb blend. You'll find it in specialist spice shops, or online at thespiceshop.co.uk.

ROAST LAMB PIE

USE UP
LEFTOVERS

BARBECOA BURGER

JAMIE'S FAVOURITE

BARBECOA BURGER

Makes 1

- ½ onion, finely sliced
- Olive oil
- A splash of Old Speckled Hen, or other strong ale
- 1–2 anchovy fillets
- 1 heaped tbsp mayonnaise
- 230g minced beef (higher fat content will give a better flavour)
- 1 heaped tbsp French's mustard, or your favourite sort
- 2 smoked streaky bacon rashers, halved
- 1 sesame seed bun, split
- 40g grated Westcombe or other nice cheddar

1 In a pan over a low-medium heat, slowly fry the onion in a little olive oil until golden and sticky. Finish with a splash of ale, stirring till evaporated. While that's going, bash your anchovies using a mortar and pestle, or slice them very finely. When they're all mashed up, mix with the mayonnaise and set aside.
2 Season the minced beef with salt and pepper and shape into a thick burger patty. Heat a small amount of oil on a hot grill pan or frying pan. Add the beef patty. Leave to seal on one side and brush the top with half the mustard. Once sealed, turn the burger and repeat with the mustard. When sealed on the bottom, turn again to get a good crust.
3 Meanwhile, fry the bacon till crisp and lightly toast the bun halves. Top the burger with the onion, bacon and cheese. Dot mayo on the base of the bun, then carefully transfer the burger with its toppings to the base. Top with the other bun half. Return the burger to the char-grill or frying pan. Place a small amount of water in the pan and use a metal bowl or cloche to cover the burger. Cook till the water has evaporated – the steam will give you a great shine on the bun!
4 Now your burger is ready to serve with pickled onions, chillies, ketchup, extra mustard – whatever you fancy!

STEAK & SAKE WITH SOBA NOODLES

STEAK & SAKE WITH SOBA NOODLES

Serves 2

- 1 x 300g sirloin steak
- 1 packet of soba noodles (about 250g)
- ½ bunch of coriander, leaves picked

Marinade

- 1 tsp wasabi paste
- 1 tbsp each of worcestershire sauce, soy sauce and sesame oil
- A pinch of chilli flakes

Sake sauce

- 60ml sake
- 1 tbsp soy sauce
- 1 tsp fish sauce
- A dash of worcestershire sauce
- 1 tsp wasabi paste

1 Mix the marinade ingredients and coat the steak. Leave to marinate for 30 minutes at room temperature.

2 Bring a pot of salted water to the boil to cook the noodles. Meanwhile, place a heavy frying pan over a high heat. When it's screaming hot, cook the steak for about 2 minutes each side for medium-rare, or until done to your liking. Transfer the steak to a warm plate, loosely cover with foil and leave to rest. Reduce the heat under the pan.
3 Cook the noodles according to packet instructions. For the sauce, pour the sake in the frying pan and bring to the boil. Once the alcohol has evaporated, add the rest of the sauce ingredients and the steak's resting juices.
4 Carve the steak into thin slices. Drain the noodles and toss with some of the sauce. Divide the noodles between 2 plates, top with the sliced steak and spoon over the remaining sauce. Scatter with coriander leaves, to serve.

SIMPLE DAUBE

BEEF RED CURRY

VENISON STEAK-FRITES

You can make this recipe with fillet steak and it will be meltingly tender. However, haunch steak is cheaper and has a great texture.

Serves 2

- 1 garlic clove, peeled
- 1 dried red chilli
- 2 rosemary sprigs, leaves picked
- Grated zest of ½ orange or 1 lemon
- Olive oil
- 2 x 175g venison haunch steaks
- English mustard and cranberry sauce or redcurrant jelly, to serve

Shoestring fries

- 500g baking potatoes, sliced into strips with a julienne cutter
- 1 litre vegetable oil, for deep-frying

1 Use a pestle to bash the garlic in a mortar with a pinch of salt until creamy, then crumble in the chilli. Add the rosemary leaves and a good pinch of pepper, then the orange or lemon zest. Bash it all up into a paste and then thin down with a good drizzle or 2 of olive oil. Place the steak in a bowl or sealable bag, pour in the marinade, massage it in with clean hands and marinate for 20 minutes, or for up to 8 hours chilled.
2 When you're ready to cook, prepare the fries. Pat the potato strips with kitchen paper so they're as dry as

possible. Heat the oil in a large saucepan and preheat a griddle over a high heat.
3 Grill the steaks for 2–3 minutes each side for rare (or to your taste), then leave to rest while you cook the fries. Very carefully, in batches if necessary, deep-fry the potatoes for 5 minutes, or until cooked through. Drain on kitchen paper and sprinkle with salt. Serve the steak-frites with mustard and cranberry sauce or redcurrant jelly.

SIMPLE DAUBE

Serves 4

- 750g braising steak
- 2 tsp herbes de Provence
- 3 thick strips of orange zest
- ½ tsp fennel seeds
- 200g smoked bacon pieces
- A glass of red wine
- 3 garlic cloves, chopped
- 1 x 400g tin tomatoes, drained

1 Preheat the oven to 140C/gas 1. Place the steak in a casserole with the herbes de Provence, orange zest and fennel seeds, then season well. In a separate pan, fry the bacon until it begins to brown, then add to the casserole. Deglaze the pan with the wine. Add the garlic and tomatoes. Use the back of a wooden spoon to break the tomatoes up, and let cook for a few minutes.

2 Pour the tomato mixture over the meat then cover the casserole tightly with a lid or foil and cook in the oven for about 2½ hours or until the meat is tender. Delicious with bread, pasta or rice and a green salad.

BEEF RED CURRY

Serves 2

- 300g rump steak, cut into 2cm strips
- 1 tsp chilli powder
- ½ tsp turmeric
- Groundnut oil
- 2 garlic cloves, sliced
- A knob of ginger, sliced
- 1 red chilli, finely sliced
- A few curry leaves
- 200g coconut milk
- A handful of beansprouts
- Noodles and lime, to serve

1 Mix the steak, chilli powder and turmeric in a bowl and season well. Heat a glug of oil in a frying pan over a high heat, add the garlic, ginger and chilli and fry for 1 minute. Stir in the curry leaves and fry for 1 minute. Add the steak, cook for a few minutes, then pour in the coconut milk. Bring to the boil and cook for 5 minutes, adding a little water. Stir in the beansprouts, cook until heated through, then serve the curry with noodles and lime.

PULLED BRISKET CHILLI

scrunch in the tomatoes, picking out any big bits of skin. Grate in the chillies, mix well and adjust seasoning. To serve, make wraps with the tortillas, brisket chilli, guacamole, yoghurt and salad.

THE ULTIMATE PORK BELLY SARNIE
Serves 8
- 2 litres apple juice
- 1 tbsp white pepper
- 1kg pork belly, in 1.5cm slices
- 2 large baguettes, sliced lengthways
- 8 tbsp fat-free plain yoghurt
- 4 tbsp English mustard
- ½ bunch of thyme
- Chilli jam, to glaze
- 1 eating apple, sliced into matchsticks

Apple sauce
- 4 bramley apples, peeled, cored and roughly chopped
- 2 tsp sugar
- 2 handfuls of watercress, half finely chopped, half torn

1 Pour the juice into a deep roasting tray. Add the pepper and a few large pinches of sea salt. Submerge the pork and refrigerate overnight, or at least 6 hours.
2 For the sauce, put apples, sugar and a splash of water in a saucepan. Bring to the boil, then simmer for 8–10 minutes, or till the apples are soft. Cool, then stir in the chopped watercress. Set aside.
3 Drain the pork and pat dry with kitchen paper. Firmly, but not roughly, flatten out the sides to increase the surface area and help it get super crisp while cooking. Skewer the meat as in the photo (right). Cook over a medium heat on a barbecue or griddle pan, in batches if need be, for 15 minutes or till charred and cooked through. Turn often.
4 Meanwhile, spoon yoghurt on cut sides of the bread. Add dollops of mustard and swirl into the yoghurt. Add some apple sauce, then the torn watercress.
5 When the pork is golden, use the thyme as a brush to spread it with chilli jam. Keep brushing and turning to create a crust. Once the pork is cooked, slice into chunks, between the skewers, then pull off with a fork and pile onto the bread halves. Scatter over the apple and spoon over extra sauce. Pop on the bread tops and quarter each baguette.

PULLED BRISKET CHILLI
Serves about 20
- 1.5kg beef brisket
- 1 large cinnamon stick
- 1 tbsp ground cumin
- 1 tbsp smoked paprika
- 1 heaped tbsp dried oregano
- Olive oil
- 2 bay leaves
- 2 red peppers
- 2 yellow peppers
- 2 x 400g tins chopped tomatoes
- 400ml beef stock
- 3-4 red chillies, 2 deseeded, all sliced
- 2 red onions, finely sliced
- Red wine vinegar
- ½ bunch of coriander, chopped
- Soft tortillas, Greek-style yoghurt and green salad, to serve

Guacamole
- 6 ripe avocados, peeled and stoned
- 1 bunch of coriander, leaves torn
- 1 small red onion, finely grated
- Juice of 4–5 limes
- 4 perfectly ripe tomatoes (different colours if you can), roughly chopped
- 1–2 red chillies, deseeded

1 Place the beef on a board and score one side. Bash the cinnamon, cumin, paprika and oregano with a mortar and pestle. Rub into the cuts in the beef. Season well, drizzle over a little olive oil and brown the brisket well in a large frying pan over a high heat.
2 Place the bay, peppers, tomatoes and stock in a large pot and bring to the boil.
3 Meanwhile, add the chilli and onion to the pan with the brisket, and cook for 5 minutes. Transfer it all to the large pot, cover and simmer for 4–4½ hours.
4 Gently pull apart the beef with 2 forks. Remove the bay, add vinegar to taste, add the coriander and adjust seasoning.
5 For the guacamole, put the avocado flesh in a bowl with the coriander, red onion and lime juice. Season, then

THE ULTIMATE PORK BELLY SARNIE

POMEGRANATE & BLUE CHEESE STEAK

POMEGRANATE & BLUE CHEESE STEAK

Serves 2
- 1 banana shallot, finely chopped
- Olive oil
- 1 tbsp pomegranate molasses
- 2 tbsp pomegranate juice
- 2 tbsp red wine
- 2 tbsp beef or chicken stock
- 2 x 200g fillet steaks, 2cm thick
- 50g roquefort or other
  blue cheese, sliced or crumbled

1 In a medium frying pan, sauté the shallot in a little olive oil until golden. Add the pomegranate molasses and juice, wine and stock. Season to taste. Simmer until reduced and a bit sticky, lowering the heat if needed.
2 Meanwhile, oil and season the steaks. Cook on a hot griddle for 2–3 minutes each side for medium-rare, or to your liking. After you've turned the steaks, top with cheese and serve with sauce.

ACHIOTE RECADO PORK & CHILLI ONION RINGS

Serves 6
- 6 pork chops
Achiote recado
- 2 tbsp annatto seeds
- 4 garlic cloves, unpeeled
- 1 onion, cut into 8 wedges
- 1 tbsp ground allspice
- 1 tbsp coriander seeds
- 1 tbsp ground cinnamon
- 1 tbsp cumin seeds
- 1 tbsp dried oregano
- 1 tsp saffron threads
- 2 tbsp ancho chilli powder or
  other Mexican chilli powder
- 200ml orange juice
- Juice of 2 limes
- 50ml cider vinegar
Chilli onion rings
- 6 tbsp flour
- 6 tbsp chilli powder or paprika
- Vegetable oil, for deep-frying
- 2 large onions, very thinly sliced

1 For the recado, place the annatto in a small saucepan, cover with a small cupful of cold water, bring to the boil then simmer gently for 20 minutes. Remove from the heat and allow the seeds to steep for a few hours. Drain in a colander, reserving the liquid.
2 Preheat the oven to 200C/gas 6. Place the garlic and onion in a small roasting tin and roast for 45 minutes or until soft. Transfer to a plate, let cool, then remove the garlic skins. Roughly chop the garlic and onion on a wooden board.
3 Place the onion mixture in a food processor with the drained annatto, allspice, coriander seeds, cinnamon, cumin seeds, oregano, saffron, chilli powder and 1 tablespoon of sea salt and blend to a rough paste. Add the orange and lime juice, cider vinegar and about 4 tablespoons of the reserved annatto liquid then blend briefly again to combine. Transfer the mixture to a large nonreactive bowl.
4 Place the pork chops in the marinade, cover with clingfilm and marinate for 3–4 hours or overnight in the fridge.
5 Remove the pork chops from the fridge and bring to room temperature. Preheat a barbecue or cast-iron griddle pan to a medium heat. Cook the pork chops, turning once, for 6-10 minutes each side depending on thickness, occasionally adding some more marinade with a brush during cooking. When cooked through, move the pork chops to a board and leave them to rest for a couple of minutes.
6 For the onion rings, place the flour and chilli powder in a large bowl, season well and mix to combine. Very carefully heat the oil in a large saucepan to 180C (always be alert when deep-frying). Place the onion slices, in batches, in the flour and coat well. Shake off the excess flour and carefully lower the onion slices into the oil. Cook for 1-2 minutes, in batches, until golden brown. Remove with a slotted spoon, then drain on kitchen paper while you cook the remaining onions.
7 Transfer the onions to a serving bowl and serve them with the pork chops, either whole or cut into smaller pieces.

RABBIT WITH POTATO & CIDER GRATIN

RABBIT WITH POTATO & CIDER GRATIN

Serves 4-6

- 2 rabbits, each cut into 6 portions
- 2 tbsp butter
- 4 red onions, quartered
- 4 garlic cloves, thinly sliced
- ½ bunch of thyme, leaves picked
- 4 tomatoes, peeled and chopped
- 500g mixed mushrooms
- 400ml cider
- 200ml chicken stock
- 2 tbsp crème fraîche

Potato & cider gratin

- 50g butter, plus extra for greasing
- 1kg potatoes, finely sliced
- 3 garlic cloves, finely sliced
- 1 tbsp thyme leaves
- 2 tbsp crème fraîche
- A small bottle or can of cider

1 Preheat the oven to 180C/gas 4. Season the rabbit pieces with salt and pepper. Melt most of the butter in a pan and brown the meat in batches. Transfer the meat to a plate and set aside. Add the remaining butter to the pan, followed by the onions, garlic and thyme. Stir and cook over a low heat for 10 minutes, till softened. Add the tomatoes and cook for 5 minutes, then add the mushrooms and cook for 3 minutes or until they are soft. Return the rabbit to the pan, pour over the cider and stock and bring to the boil. Put 3 or 4 sheets of greaseproof paper on top, then the lid. Simmer for 45-60 minutes.
2 Meanwhile, for the gratin, grease a 24cm x 20cm baking dish. Add a layer of potatoes, some slices of garlic, a few thyme leaves and a few dots of butter and crème fraîche. Season well, add a small splash of cider and top with more potatoes. Continue layering until everything, except the cider, is used. Dot the top with butter and a sprinkling of salt and place in the oven. Cooking time depends on the depth of the dish. Check the gratin after 40 minutes; if it's browning too much but not cooked through, cover with foil and cook for up to 90 minutes, till the potatoes are done.
3 When the rabbit is tender, check the seasoning and adjust if necessary. For a thicker sauce, remove the rabbit from the pan and simmer the sauce, without a lid, over a high heat for 5-10 minutes.

Stir in the crème fraîche then return the rabbit to the pan. Cooking times vary, so either the gratin or stew might be done earlier than the other. If so, cover with foil and keep warm till the other is done.

PRESSURE COOKING

BEEF BRISKET WITH WINE & SHALLOTS

BEEF BRISKET WITH WINE & SHALLOTS

Serves 8

- 2 tbsp extra-virgin olive oil
- 1.5kg beef brisket, rolled and tied
- 12 shallots, peeled
- 6 garlic cloves, peeled
- 1 x 400g tin chopped tomatoes
- 2 tbsp tomato purée
- 250ml red wine
- 2 bay leaves
- 1 cinnamon stick
- ¼ whole nutmeg, grated
- A small handful of black olives
- 1 tsp dried oregano
- A few thyme sprigs
- 2 tbsp red wine vinegar

1 Heat the olive oil in a pressure cooker. Add the beef and turn it every couple of minutes until it is golden on all sides. Remove and set aside.
2 Add shallots and garlic to the cooker and fry for around 10 minutes, until they start to soften and take on colour, then add all the remaining ingredients except the beef. Half-fill the tomato tin with water and tip this in. Season, and gently stir until hot and thickening.
3 Return the beef to the pan and put the lid on, making sure the valve is shut. Cook at a low heat for 1¼ hours. Release the valve and, once the steam has stopped hissing, remove the lid. Leave the beef to rest for 10 minutes before removing. If it is not tender enough, you can always put the cooker back on to pressure again and cook for 15 more minutes. It should flake easily with 2 forks. Stir the remaining sauce and season. Break apart or carve the beef and serve with the sauce on top.

ITALIAN-STYLE STUFFED LAMB

OXTAIL STEW

Oxtail is an ingredient that's coming back into vogue. Orange, dates and spices lend sweetness and fragrance.
Serves 8
- 50g flour
- 2.5kg trimmed oxtail, cut into rounds
- Olive oil
- 500g shallots, finely diced
- 3 garlic cloves, sliced
- 1 tsp ground cloves
- 5-7.5cm piece of ginger, grated
- A pinch of ground nutmeg
- Peeled zest of 1 large orange, or 2-3 strips of dried orange peel
- 1 punnet of medjool or other soft dates, stoned
- Balsamic or sherry vinegar, to taste
Braised kale
- 1 large bunch of kale
- 3 thick streaky bacon rashers, diced
- 1 garlic clove, thinly sliced
- 1 chilli (or to taste), finely chopped

1 Preheat the oven to 200C/gas 6. Season the flour, then use to dredge the oxtail till well coated. Shake off any excess flour and set the meat aside.
2 Heat 2 tablespoons of oil in a large shallow frying pan over a low-medium heat. Gently cook the shallots and garlic until fragrant but not coloured. Transfer to a large ovenproof dish and set aside.
3 Heat 2-3 tablespoons more oil in the same pan over a medium-high heat. Fry the oxtail, in batches if necessary, until well browned all over. Pack the oxtail over the shallots and garlic. Add the cloves, ginger, nutmeg and orange peel and cover with 2-3cm of water.
4 Place in the oven and cook for 15 minutes, then reduce the heat to 140C/gas 1 and cook for 2½ hours, or until the meat is just tender. Check the liquid from time to time, adding water if needed. Season. Add the dates and vinegar. Cook for 30 more minutes or until the dates are plump.
5 Meanwhile, blanch the kale in salted boiling water for 3-4 minutes then drain. Fry the bacon with the garlic till cooked, turn off the heat and stir in the chilli. Add the kale and stir to combine.
6 Remove the dish from the oven and skim off the excess fat. Serve each person some oxtail with a few dates, some of the pan juices and a bit of kale.

ITALIAN-STYLE STUFFED LAMB

If you can find them (try good delis), use grilled artichoke hearts marinated in oil. They hold their shape better
Serves 8-10
- 1 x 2.4kg leg of lamb, boned and butterflied
- 120g pecorino romano, sliced into triangles
- 5-6 grilled artichoke hearts
- 14 anchovy fillets, drained
- 2 tbsp each roughly chopped mint, rosemary and flat-leaf parsley
- 2 tbsp coarse breadcrumbs
- 2 tbsp olive oil

1 Preheat the oven to its highest temperature. Place the lamb flat on a board and lay the pecorino on top.
2 Flatten the artichoke hearts with the ball of your hand, then layer them over the pecorino. Place the anchovy fillets on top, followed by the mint, rosemary, parsley and breadcrumbs. Season generously with sea salt and freshly ground black pepper and drizzle with 1 tablespoon of olive oil.
3 Using both hands, firmly roll up the lamb from the short end, so it ends up in the shape of a swiss roll. Tie up the meat tightly with kitchen string at 3cm intervals. Transfer to a roasting tin and drizzle with the remaining olive oil. Add 50ml water to the tin and roast the lamb for 20 minutes, then reduce the heat to 160C/gas 2½ and roast for another 90 minutes. Allow the lamb to rest for 10 minutes before carving it into thick slices. Serve hot or cold.

OXTAIL STEW

PLUM-GLAZED GAMMON

GREAT FOR XMAS

PLUM-GLAZED GAMMON

Serves 10-12 with leftovers

- 3kg gammon joint
- 1 tbsp black peppercorns
- 1 onion, cut into wedges
- 1 bouquet garni (leek, celery, bay and thyme tied with kitchen string)
- About 100g plum jam
- ½-1 tsp chilli flakes
- White wine vinegar
- Cranberry sauce, sliced apples, mint and chilli, to serve

1 Preheat the oven to 160C/gas 2½. Put the gammon in a roasting tray with the peppercorns, onion and bouquet garni and half-fill the pan with water. Cover with foil and roast for 1½ hours or till pink and cooked through, then remove and cool, covered, for 20-30 minutes.
2 Once cool enough to handle, remove the skin (retaining some of the fat underneath) and diagonally score the meat with a sharp knife.
3 Put the gammon back in the oven and roast at 200C/gas 6 for 30 minutes to crisp the fat. Remove from the oven, brush with a little jam to glaze and sprinkle with chilli flakes. Continue cooking for 30-40 minutes, glazing every 10 minutes or so till crisp, golden and sticky. When the gammon is cooked to your liking, transfer to a board to rest.
4 Add a good splash of vinegar to the tray and stir to deglaze. Taste; add some plum jam if too sharp. Serve gammon with pan juices, cranberry sauce and a salad of sliced apples, mint and chilli.

INDIVIDUAL CHORIZO PIES

Recipe by Andy Bates
Serves 8

- 1 red onion, halved
- 1 small fennel bulb, halved
- 1 red pepper, halved and deseeded
- 1 tbsp olive oil
- Sweet smoked paprika
- 300g chorizo, very finely chopped
- 500g pork mince

INDIVIDUAL CHORIZO PIES

Hot-water crust pastry
- 450g flour
- ½ tsp salt
- 170g lard or butter, melted
- 200ml water
- 3 egg yolks, beaten

1 Using a food processor, mandolin or very sharp knife, finely chop the vegetables. Add the oil to a pan over a low-medium heat and fry the onion and fennel for 5 minutes. Add the pepper and a pinch of paprika. Continue to fry gently for 30 minutes, until the veg start to darken. Allow to cool.
2 Add the chorizo and pork mince to the vegetables, mix thoroughly and season. Divide the mixture into 8 portions and refrigerate while you make the pastry.
3 Preheat the oven to 200C/gas 6 and line a baking tray with greaseproof paper. For the pastry, mix the flour and salt in a bowl and make a well in the centre. Bring the lard and water to the

boil in a saucepan, then stir into the flour with a wooden spoon to form a smooth dough. Leave the pastry for 5 minutes if it is too hot to handle.
4 Place the pastry on a floured surface and roll out to about 5mm thick. Place the meat portions on the pastry and cut a circle around each one that's double its size, to ensure you can then wrap the pastry all around the filling, pinching and smoothing to create a ball. The filling should now be totally wrapped in pastry with no holes or gaps.
5 Using a pastry cutter, cut 8 small circles from the remaining dough, brush with the beaten egg yolk and place on top of the pies to create 'lids'.
6 Place the pies on the baking tray and brush with more egg yolk to give the pies a lovely golden finish when cooked. With a knife, make a small hole in each lid to allow air to escape while cooking. Bake for 35 minutes until golden and oozing chorizo juice. Eat hot or cold.

Adeline Boyd
24 from Tooting

Jack Wells
22 from Camberwell

Charles Aston
20 from Camden Town

Dong Tran
23 from Old Ford

Billy Brennan
21 from Plumstead

Congratulations class of 2011

Fifteen London is a restaurant that uses the magic of food to give unemployed young people a chance to have a better future. All profits from the restaurant go to the Jamie Oliver Foundation, which funds a pioneering Apprentice Programme. Pictured are Fifteen London's most recent graduates. They've received a Level 2 in Professional Cookery from college and training in the Fifteen kitchens, taking in everything from traditional bakery and butchery to the finest pastry skills. It costs a lot to train each apprentice. But it's worth it, not only to the apprentices, but to society as a whole. Our ambitions are bigger than our budgets and, quite simply, we need help from everyone who believes that what we're doing is a good idea. Please support our Apprentice Programme with a donation – visit www.virginmoneygiving.com and search 'Jamie Oliver Foundation'. Thank you! Alternatively, book a table at Fifteen London; call **0203 375 1515** or visit **www.fifteen.net**

FIFTEEN
LONDON

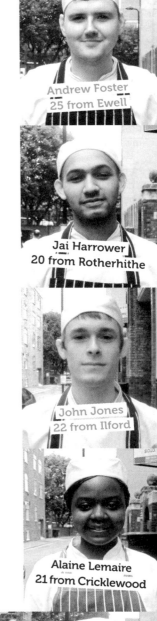

Andrew Foster
25 from Ewell

Jai Harrower
20 from Rotherhithe

John Jones
22 from Ilford

Alaine Lemaire
21 from Cricklewood

Janek Flemyng
20 from Clapton

Emma Ogoe
21 from Ilford

Mercy Taembo
21 from Custom House

Oliver Quelch
25 from Camden Town

Katie Opher
25 from Catford

DESSERTS

RHUBARB & CUSTARD FAIRY CAKES

RHUBARB & CUSTARD FAIRY CAKES

Makes 12
- 300g rhubarb, sliced into 1cm pieces, plus one trimmed stalk to decorate
- 125g sugar, plus 7 tbsp extra
- Grated zest and juice of 1 orange
- 100ml plain yoghurt
- 2 eggs
- 100g self-raising flour
- ½ tsp baking powder
- 75g ground almonds

Custard icing
- 200ml milk
- 2 tbsp cornflour
- 175g butter
- 175g sugar
- 2 tbsp mascarpone
- 1 tsp vanilla extract

1 Preheat the oven to 180C/gas 4 and line a cupcake tray with 12 cases. Add the rhubarb to a small saucepan with 4 tablespoons of sugar and a squeeze of orange juice, bring to the boil, then reduce the heat and simmer for 2 minutes to soften – but not stew – the rhubarb. Remove the fruit with a slotted spoon to drain the liquid and set aside. Leave to cool.
2 Beat the yoghurt and eggs together in a bowl. In a separate bowl, mix the flour, baking powder, 125g sugar, orange zest, ground almonds and a pinch of salt until combined. Make a well in the centre and lightly stir in the yoghurt mixture. Fold through the rhubarb then spoon the mixture into the 12 cupcake cases and bake for 18–20 minutes, or until golden and cooked through. Remove the cakes from the oven and leave to cool.
3 Meanwhile, make the custard icing. Mix a splash of milk with the cornflour to form a paste. Heat the remaining milk in a saucepan over a medium heat, then whisk into the cornflour paste and return it all to the pan. Cook over a low heat, stirring constantly, until thick, then remove from the heat and cool.
4 Cream together the butter, sugar, mascarpone and a pinch of salt in a bowl until pale. Beat in the cooled milk mixture and vanilla extract, then use to ice the cooled cupcakes.
5 To decorate, slice the remaining rhubarb into 2–3mm rounds. Sprinkle with 3 tbsp sugar, toss on a plate and then place on top of the cakes.

FIG & OLIVE OIL CAKE

Serves 8
- 200g flour
- 125g ground almonds
- 1 tbsp baking powder
- 300g caster sugar
- 3 eggs
- Grated zest of 1 lemon
- Grated zest and juice of 2 oranges
- 125ml extra-virgin olive oil
- 100ml milk
- 4 figs, halved
- 3 tbsp honey

1 Preheat the oven to 180C/gas 4 and line a 20cm x 12cm loaf tin. Place the flour, almonds and baking powder in a bowl and mix together.
2 In a separate bowl, whisk the sugar and eggs until fluffy. Add the citrus zest and juice, then stir in the oil and milk. Gently fold in the flour mixture then pour the batter into the prepared tin and bake in the oven for 40 minutes.
3 Push the figs into the top of the loaf. Drizzle with honey and bake for 15–20 minutes, until the top is caramelised and a skewer inserted comes out clean. Cool, then remove from the tin.

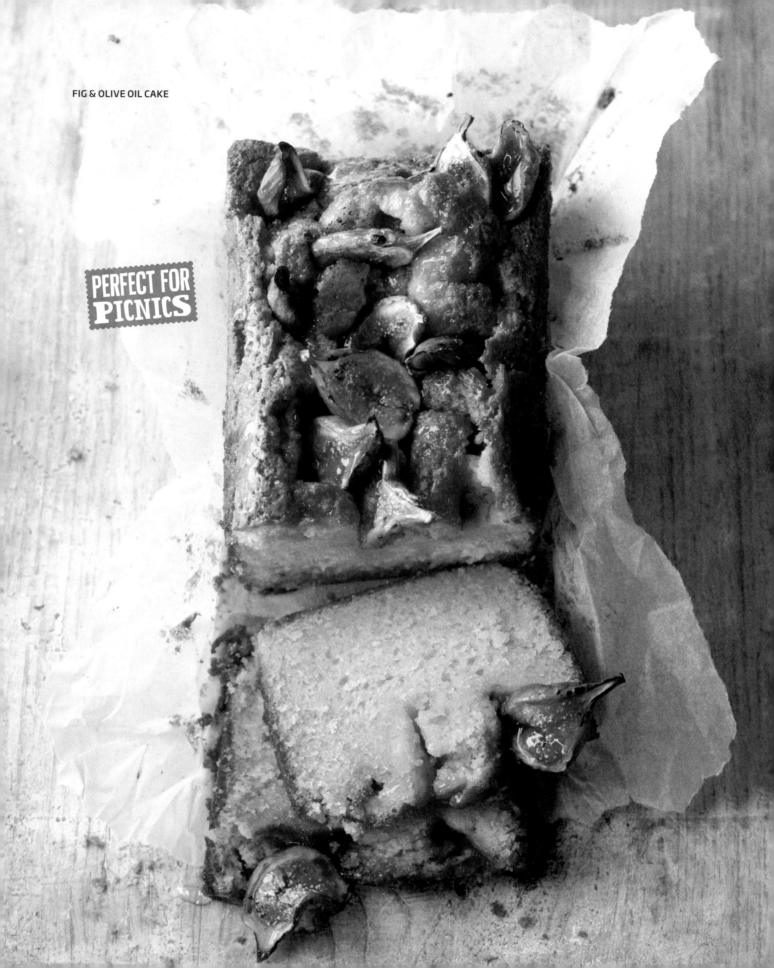

FIG & OLIVE OIL CAKE

PERFECT FOR PICNICS

PLUM RIPPLE ICE CREAM

Get the scoop

Think outside the tub when it comes to using ice cream in recipes. Make ice cream sandwiches by spreading it between soft choc-chip cookies and refreezing briefly. Try vanilla with ginger biscuits or coffee between chocolate digestives. Make an arctic roll by baking a flat sponge cake and rolling it around ice cream that's had fruit and nuts added to it, then refreezing to firm up. Try lining a loaf tin with clingfilm and layering ice cream up with crushed biscuits and nuts, ice cream and dried fruit. Refreeze, remove from the tin and slice to serve. Make a banana split by splitting a banana and filling it with 3 different ice-cream flavours, then top with whipped cream, crushed nuts and cherries. And for an American-style ice-cream soda, place a little fruit in syrup or chocolate in a glass, then add a few scoops of ice cream and top with a little fizzy water.

ALMOND & HONEY ICE CREAM

DAIRY FREE

PLUM RIPPLE ICE CREAM

Makes about 1.5 litres

- 3 plums
- 150g sugar
- 500ml double cream
- 500ml milk
- 1 vanilla pod
- 7 egg yolks

1 Place the plums in a saucepan with 30g sugar and a splash of water and cook over a medium heat until soft. Press through a sieve and let cool.
2 Place the cream, milk and vanilla pod in a pan over a medium heat, bring to just under the boil, then reduce the heat to low. Beat the egg yolks and remaining sugar together until frothy. Slowly pour the hot milk mixture over the egg mixture, whisking constantly.
3 Cover with clingfilm and allow to cool, then pour into an ice-cream machine and churn according to manufacturer's instructions. When finished, stir the plum mixture through to create a ripple effect, then freeze until needed.

ALMOND & HONEY ICE CREAM

Makes about 1.5 litres

- 500ml almond milk
- 500ml hazelnut milk
- 4 tbsp sugar
- 4 tbsp honey
- 500g soya yoghurt
- A splash of amaretto (optional)

1 Place the almond and hazelnut milks, sugar and honey in a saucepan and simmer over a low heat until the sugar has dissolved – don't let it boil. Allow the mixture to cool, then whisk in the soya yoghurt and amaretto, if using.
2 Place the mixture in an ice-cream maker and churn according to the manufacturer's instructions, until thick and frozen. Remove to a medium bowl or freezer-proof container and freeze for at least 1 hour to set. This is lovely scattered with crushed toasted almonds.

LEMON VERBENA SORBET

Not pictured
Makes about 600ml

- 15g lemon verbena leaves
- 1 mint sprig, leaves picked
- 175g sugar
- Zest of ½ lemon and juice of 1
- 1 tbsp limoncello

1 In a processor, blitz the herbs, sugar and zest until finely chopped. Transfer to a jug and pour in the juice, limoncello and 600ml water. Mix until the sugar dissolves. Let infuse for a few hours, strain, then churn in an ice-cream maker. For a treat, scoop into champagne flutes and top with prosecco.

ETON MESS CAKE

CHOC-MINT LAYER CAKE
Serves 16
- 100g butter, at room temperature
- 200g sugar
- 2 eggs, beaten
- ½ tbsp vanilla extract
- 4 heaped tbsp cocoa powder
- 300g flour
- 250ml buttermilk
- 1 tsp bicarbonate of soda
- 1 tbsp white wine vinegar

Mint icing
- 100g butter
- 400g icing sugar
- 200g low-fat cream cheese
- 2½ tbsp milk
- ¼–½ tsp mint extract
- ½–1 tsp green food dye (optional)
- 8 mint chocolate thins, crushed

1 Preheat the oven to 180C/gas 4 and grease and line two 23cm round cake tins. Cream the butter and sugar together until light and fluffy. Gradually mix in the eggs with a good pinch of salt and stir in the vanilla extract.
2 In another bowl, mix together the cocoa powder and flour, then add half to the butter mixture. Mix well, then add 125ml buttermilk. Fold in the remaining flour mixture to the butter mixture and mix well, then stir in the remaining buttermilk.
3 In a small bowl, mix the bicarbonate of soda and vinegar so they froth up, then stir into the cake batter. Divide between the 2 tins and bake for 25–30 minutes, or until a skewer inserted into the centre comes out clean. Leave to cool in the tins, then turn out and slice each cake in half horizontally.
4 For the icing, cream the butter and icing sugar in a large bowl until smooth. Gradually beat in the cream cheese, and then the milk. Mix in the mint extract and the food dye, if using. Layer the sponges, spreading a quarter of the icing and a scattering of crushed mint chocolate thins between each layer. Finish with a layer of mint icing and sprinkle over the mint chocolate thins.

ETON MESS CAKE
Serves 10
- 125g butter, plus extra for greasing
- 300g sugar, plus 1 tbsp extra
- 4 eggs, separated
- Finely grated zest of 1 lemon and a squeeze of juice
- 125g self-raising flour
- ½ tsp baking powder
- 2 tbsp milk
- 225g strawberries, hulled and sliced
- 1 vanilla pod, split lengthways, seeds scraped
- 150ml double cream
- 3 tbsp strawberry jam
- Icing sugar, to serve

1 Preheat the oven to 200C/gas 6 and grease and line two 20cm round cake tins. Cream the butter and 100g sugar until pale. Beat in the egg yolks, lemon zest, flour and baking powder. Fold in the milk, then divide the cake batter between the 2 prepared tins.

2 In a clean bowl, whisk the egg whites until soft peaks form, then gradually whisk in the remaining 200g sugar. Keep mixing for about 5 minutes, until the whites are glossy and stiff. Place a handful of the strawberries in a bowl, add a squeeze of lemon juice and 1 tablespoon of sugar and then mash with the back of a fork until puréed. Ripple the purée into the meringue then divide between the 2 tins, peaking one of the meringues with a fork. Bake for 20–25 minutes until cooked through and a skewer inserted comes out clean. Leave to cool in the tins.
3 Meanwhile, add the vanilla seeds to the cream and whisk until soft peaks form. When both the cakes are cool, transfer the unpeaked cake to a cake stand or wooden board, spoon over the jam, scatter with the remaining sliced strawberries, spoon over the cream, then top with the remaining cake. Dust with icing sugar just before serving.

CHOC-MINT LAYER CAKE

MANGO TART

MANGO TART

Recipe by Sue Fairlie-Cuninghame

Serves 8

- 2 ripe mangoes
- Sugar, to caramelise

Pastry

- 250g flour
- 50g ground almonds
- 75g sugar
- 175g chilled butter, diced
- 1 egg
- 1 tsp vanilla extract

Crème patisserie

- 125ml milk
- 35g sugar
- ½ tsp vanilla extract
- 2 egg yolks
- 1 tsp cornflour
- 1 tsp flour
- 125ml double cream, whipped

1 For the pastry, blitz the flour, almonds, sugar and butter in a food processor until the mixture resembles coarse breadcrumbs. Beat the egg with the vanilla and 1 tablespoon of cold water then add to the processor and pulse until the pastry forms a ball. Wrap in clingfilm and chill for 1–2 hours.
2 Preheat the oven to 180C/gas 4. Roll the pastry out to 5mm thick and use to line a 35cm x 11cm x 3cm flan tin. Line the pastry with 4 layers of clingfilm, fill with dried beans and blind bake until just golden. Cool and store in an airtight container until ready to use.
3 For the crème patisserie, place the milk, sugar and vanilla in a pan and bring to a simmer. Whisk the yolks in a bowl until creamy, sprinkle over the flours, then pour the milk mixture into the yolk mixture, whisking. Return to the pan and cook for 2–3 minutes, until the flours are cooked and the mixture has thickened. Transfer to a bowl, cover and chill. Once cold, fold through the whipped cream. Keep chilled.
4 Carefully peel the mangoes, slice off the cheeks and thinly slice, horizontally. Just before serving, spread the crème patisserie inside the tart case. Lay the mango slices on a board, sprinkle with sugar and, using a blowtorch or hot metal spoon, caramelise the sugar. Lay mango on the crème patisserie.

LEMON CREPE CAKE

LEMON CREPE CAKE

This delightfully tangy cake is easy to make and looks very impressive. It's very rich, so serve it in thin slices.

Serves 16

- 21 large readymade crêpes (available from supermarkets)
- 6 tsp gelatine powder
- 4 x 320g jars of lemon curd
- Grated zest of 1 lemon and crème fraîche, to serve

Candied lemon slices

- 190g granulated sugar
- 1 lemon, thinly sliced
- 6 drops of lemon essence

1 For the candied lemon, place the sugar in a pan with 200ml cold water and heat until the sugar dissolves. Add the lemon slices and essence, cover the surface with baking paper, reduce the heat to low and simmer for 30 minutes, or until the lemon is almost translucent. Remove from the heat, leave to cool, then remove the candied lemon slices to a wire rack over a tray (reserving the syrup) and set aside.
2 Place 200ml boiling water in a large saucepan over a low heat, sprinkle in the gelatine and whisk for 2–3 minutes, until it dissolves. Add the lemon curd and stir for a few minutes, then remove from the heat and leave to cool.
3 Line a 24cm springform cake tin with clingfilm so it overhangs the sides. Place 1 crêpe in the base of the tin and spread over 2 tablespoons of lemon curd mixture. Continue layering the crêpes and curd until you've used all the crêpes, finishing with a crêpe. Pull the clingfilm over the cake and chill overnight, or until the cake is firm.
4 Remove the cake from the tin and transfer to a stand or large plate. Top with the candied lemon slices and a drizzle of the reserved syrup, then scatter over the grated lemon zest and serve with crème fraîche.

BERRIES WITH CHEESECAKE CREAM

BERRIES WITH CHEESECAKE CREAM

Recipe by Matt Tebbutt
Serves 4

- 300g fresh blackberries
- 300g fresh blueberries
- 1-2 tbsp sugar, to taste
- Grated zest and juice of 1 orange
- A splash of Grand Marnier or other orange liqueur, if desired
- Shortbread or other biscuits, to serve (optional)

Cheesecake cream

- 75ml double cream
- 190g cream cheese
- 1 vanilla pod, split lengthways, seeds scraped, or 1-2 drops of vanilla extract
- 60g sugar
- A squeeze of lemon juice

1 Place the blackberries and blueberries in a wide saucepan with the sugar, orange zest, juice and booze, if using (if not, add a splash of water to get the heat going in the pan). When the fruit hits a very gentle bubble, immediately remove from the heat, cover the pan and allow to cool.
2 For the cheesecake cream, stir the cream into the cream cheese to loosen it. Add the vanilla seeds (or extract), sugar and lemon juice and stir together until thick and smooth.
3 Serve the berries warm or at room temperature in bowls with a dollop of the cheesecake cream, and some little biscuits, if you like.

CROUSTADE

Apple tart
Recipe by Caroline Conran

This is a Gascon apple pie, but the amazing crust is so unbelievably thin that it's called a 'wedding veil' or 'nun's veil'. Traditionally it was rolled out by hand, but readymade filo pastry makes a very good croustade and is easy to use. This pie keeps well for a day, or even two, and can be reheated.
Serves 6-8

- 1kg golden delicious or chanteclaire apples, peeled, quartered, cored and thinly sliced
- 100ml armagnac
- 55g unsalted butter, melted
- 270g filo pastry (approx 12 sheets)
- 115g sugar, plus extra to sprinkle
- 1 tsp vanilla sugar, or a few drops of vanilla extract
- Zest of 1 lemon, finely grated
- A pinch of finely chopped rosemary

1 Put the apple slices in a bowl and pour over the armagnac. Cover with clingfilm and leave in the fridge overnight.
2 Preheat the oven to 190C/gas 5. Brush a loose-based 25cm round flan tin with a little of the melted butter. Brush a sheet of pastry with butter and lay it over the bottom of the tin, draping the excess over the sides. Sprinkle over ½ teaspoon of sugar. Brush a second pastry sheet with butter and lay it at right angles to the first then sprinkle with sugar. Repeat the process with more pastry sheets, laying each sheet diagonally, until you have 4 pastry sheets remaining.
3 Drain the apple slices (but not too thoroughly as the armagnac flavour is so good!) then mix them in a bowl with the remaining sugar, vanilla extract, lemon zest and rosemary. Pile the apple slices into the flan tin and spread them out evenly. Brush the remaining pastry sheets with butter and sprinkle with sugar, as before, then drape over the apples, each sheet at right angles to the one before it. Draw the overhanging ends lightly over the top of the pie and arrange them so they stick up as much as possible, like crumpled tissue paper. They should completely cover the top of the pie, forming a light and airy crust. Brush lightly with butter.
4 Bake for 20 minutes until golden, then very loosely cover with a sheet of foil. Continue to cook for a further 20-25 minutes. Allow it to cool slightly in the tin before transferring to a serving plate. If you feel nervous about doing this, serve it from the flan tin.

POACHED RHUBARB

POACHED RHUBARB

Serves 2

- 100g sugar, plus extra
- 1 vanilla pod, split lengthways
- 400g rhubarb, in 5cm slices
- 4 tbsp yoghurt
- 2 mini brioche

1 Place the sugar in a saucepan with 300ml water and dissolve over a low heat. Add ½ vanilla pod and boil for 5 minutes then reduce the heat and add the rhubarb. Simmer for about 8 minutes, till tender. Scrape the seeds out of the other vanilla pod half and mix into the yoghurt, adding a little sugar to taste. Slice the mini brioche and lightly toast. Serve with the rhubarb and a dollop of vanilla yoghurt.

VEGAN CHOCOLATE TART WITH RHUBARB

You won't miss the dairy in this rich chocolate tart, which is beautifully offset by tangy rhubarb.

Serves 12

- 150ml soya milk
- 4 cardamom pods, crushed
- 4 tbsp sugar
- 1 tbsp cornflour
- 250g dark (70% cocoa) vegan chocolate, broken into small pieces
- 1 tsp vanilla extract

Pastry

- 125g soya margarine, chilled and cut into pieces, plus extra for greasing
- 250g flour
- 125g icing sugar
- 1 tsp ground ginger

Rhubarb

- 400g rhubarb, cut into 5cm pieces
- 2-3 tbsp sugar
- A splash of ginger cordial
- Grated zest and juice of 1 orange

1 Preheat the oven to 180C/gas 4. Lightly grease a 25cm loose-bottomed round tart tin. To make the pastry, sift the flour, icing sugar and ginger into a large bowl. Add the margarine and, working quickly, rub into the dry ingredients. Add just enough cold water so you can bring the mixture together into a ball. Wrap the dough in clingfilm and chill for 30 minutes.
2 Once chilled, roll the pastry to 5mm thick and use it to line the tin. Trim any excess and prick all over with a fork. Return to the fridge for 30 minutes. Preheat the oven to 180C/gas 4.
3 Blind bake the pastry for 15 minutes then remove the weights and cook for 10-15 minutes, until golden brown and cooked through. When cool, store in an airtight container until needed.
4 For the filling, place the soya milk in a small pan with 200ml water, the cardamom pods and sugar and warm over a low heat. Put the cornflour in a small bowl with a few tablespoons of the warm soya mixture and stir till smooth, then add to the pan, stirring to combine, and bring back to the boil.
5 Put the chocolate in a bowl and pour over the hot soya mixture through a sieve. Stir to combine. Add the vanilla extract and a pinch of salt, pour into the case, then chill for 5-6 hours.
6 To cook the rhubarb, place in an ovenproof dish with 2 or 3 tablespoons of sugar, depending on how sharp the rhubarb is. Add the ginger cordial, orange zest and juice, and cover with a disc of greaseproof-paper. Bake for 20-25 minutes until the fruit is soft but holding its shape. Leave to cool. Serve thin slices of the chocolate tart with the rhubarb on the side.

VEGAN

VEGAN CHOCOLATE TART WITH RHUBARB

CHOCOLATE POTS WITH ORANGE CARAMEL

MOELLEUX AU CHOCOLAT

CHOCOLATE & BANANA LOAF

CHOCOLATE POTS WITH ORANGE CARAMEL
Makes 4-6
- 400ml single cream
- 1 vanilla pod, split lengthways
- 100g milk chocolate, in small chunks
- 6 egg yolks
- 150g sugar
- 100g white chocolate (optional)

Orange caramel
- 250g sugar
- 2 oranges, segmented

1 For the caramel, place the sugar in a small, heavy-based pan with 150ml water. Cook, without stirring, over a low heat until the sugar is dissolved, then bring to the boil. As soon as the caramel is a mahogany colour, carefully and quickly pour in 150ml water and stir in a pinch of salt. Spoon the caramel into glasses and top with 2-3 orange segments, reserving the rest for later.
2 Place the cream and vanilla pod in a pan. Heat until nearly boiling. Add the chocolate and stir until melted. Remove from the heat and discard the vanilla pod. Beat the egg yolks with the sugar in a heatproof bowl, then pour in the chocolate mixture. Return to the pan and heat gently, stirring with a wooden spoon until the mixture coats the spoon.
3 Pour into glasses and chill for 2 hours, or till set. Serve with shavings of white chocolate and any remaining orange, if you like. You could also serve this in smaller cups with the orange segments on the side, not the bottom.

MOELLEUX AU CHOCOLAT
Serves 6
- 50g unsalted butter, at room temperature, plus extra for greasing
- 350g dark (70% cocoa) chocolate, broken into pieces
- 150g sugar
- 4 large eggs
- 1 tsp vanilla extract
- 50g flour

1 Preheat the oven to 200C/gas 6. Put a baking sheet in the oven to heat. Butter 6 ramekins or 160ml dariole moulds and line the bases with greaseproof paper.
2 Melt the chocolate over a bain marie, or bowl over simmering water, then take off the heat and let cool slightly.
3 Cream the butter and sugar together until pale and slightly fluffy. Beat in the eggs one at a time. Add the vanilla and a pinch of salt. Stir in the flour until just combined, then gently mix in the melted chocolate. The mixture should thicken. Divide between moulds and bake on the preheated baking sheet for 10 minutes. Turn out and serve.

CHOCOLATE & BANANA LOAF
This loaf is best served slightly warm, not long after baking, when the chocolate is still melted.
Makes 1 large or 2 small loaves
- 100g butter, plus extra for greasing
- 200g sugar
- 2 eggs, beaten
- 75ml milk
- 300g self-raising flour, sifted
- 1 tsp bicarbonate of soda
- ½ tsp ground cinnamon
- ½ tsp ground nutmeg
- 4 ripe bananas (about 480g with skin), peeled and mashed
- 100g dark (70% cocoa) chocolate, broken into pieces

1 Preheat the oven to 180C/gas 4. Grease 1 large or 2 small loaf tins and line with greaseproof paper.
2 Cream the butter and sugar until pale and fluffy, then gradually add the beaten eggs and milk.
3 Gently fold in the flour, bicarbonate of soda, spices and 1 teaspoon of salt, then fold in the banana and chocolate, being careful not to over-mix.
4 Pour the batter into the cake tin and bake on the middle shelf of the oven for 35-40 minutes for 2 small loaves or 45-50 minutes for a large one. Enjoy a slice with a nice cup of tea or coffee.

LYCHEES IN WINE JELLY

GROWN-UP
TREAT

The joys of jelly

Jellies are the dessert of the people – fun for kids, or an elegant finish for adults. You can create exciting variations with almost any liquid – just add gelatine to set, as per packet instructions. Some, like pineapple juice and alcohol, need more gelatine to set properly; or they can be mixed with other ingredients. Add gin to extra tonic and diluted lime cordial, then serve with berries. For a bellini jelly, mix equal parts prosecco and peach juice, then set in wine glasses. For fun kids' jellies, halve then juice oranges; reserve the halves and remove remaining flesh, so you have clean 'shells'. Make a firm jelly with the juice, then pour it into the orange halves, and cut into quarters when set. Add gelatine to rhubarb cordial (page 150) and some vanilla custard and layer them up, chilling between layers, for a stripy effect.

PIMM'S JELLY

LYCHEES IN WINE JELLY

Recipe by Sue Fairlie-Cuninghame
Serves 6-8

- 1 x 425g tin lychees
- 6 gelatine leaves
- 750ml dessert wine
- 60g sugar
- Cream, to serve (optional)

1 Drain the lychees in a colander set over a bowl. Reserve the juice. Soak the gelatine in 125ml cold water until soft.
2 Place the wine and sugar in a pan and bring to the boil, stirring constantly. Reduce the heat and simmer until the sugar has dissolved and the alcohol has evaporated. Squeeze the water from the gelatine leaves and add them to the wine mixture, stirring until dissolved. Set aside to cool a little.
3 Add the drained lychee juice to the pan, stirring to combine. Arrange the lychees evenly in a shallow 2-litre jelly mould, pour over the juice mixture, cover with clingfilm and chill for at least 4 hours or until the jelly has set.
4 To remove the jelly, invert the mould over a plate and leave it to drop out (about 5 minutes), or rub the outside of the tin with a tea towel dipped in hot water and wrung out, put a plate over the jelly and invert. Serve with a dollop of cream, if you wish.

PIMM'S JELLY

Like everyone else, we at *Jamie* like to celebrate sunny days with a Pimm's. And we love a nice jelly. Here they are together at last!
Serves 4

- 7g sachet gelatine powder
- 150ml Pimm's
- 450ml lemonade
- 2-3 mint sprigs, leaves picked
- ½ apple, cored, finely chopped
- ½ orange, sliced, finely chopped (peeled if you don't like peel's tang)
- 2-4 strawberries, finely chopped
- ¼ cucumber, finely chopped

1 Sprinkle the gelatine powder over 3 tablespoons of water to soften. Gently heat the Pimm's, lemonade and mint stalks in a pan until just starting to steam. Do not boil. Remove the mint stalks, add the softened gelatine and whisk until dissolved. Remove from the heat and leave to cool. Divide most of the fruit, cucumber and mint between 4 chilled glasses then add two-thirds of the Pimm's mixture. Chill in the fridge for 20-30 minutes, keeping the rest of the mixture at room temperature. When the jelly layer has set, add the remaining fruit and mint and top with the rest of the Pimm's mixture. Leave to set in the fridge for 2 hours.

ELDERFLOWER POSSET

the cake tin. Bake for 45–50 minutes, until a skewer inserted into the centre comes out clean. Remove the cake from the oven and leave it to cool in the tin.
2 For the syrup, place the cordial and honey in a saucepan over a medium heat and bring to the boil. Reduce the heat and simmer for 5 minutes till thickened. Taste and add a squeeze of lemon juice, if necessary. Reserve 2 tablespoons of the syrup for the icing. Make a few holes in the warm cake with a skewer then gently pour the remaining syrup over the cake. Leave the cake to cool a little in the tin then turn out onto a wire rack.
3 For the icing, mix the yoghurt, icing sugar and syrup until smooth. Spread over the cooled cake and top with a handful of chopped pistachios.

ELDERFLOWER, CUCUMBER & LIME GRANITA

Not pictured

This is summer on a spoon. We can't think of three flavours that could create a more refreshing little number than this. If you have an ice-cream maker, use it to make a smooth, refined sorbet. If not, all you need is a tray and a fork to make delicate mounds of crystals. It's best eaten within a couple of days.

Makes 1.5 litres
- 4 large cucumbers, peeled, roughly chopped
- Finely grated zest of 2 limes and juice of 6
- 500ml elderflower cordial

1 Blitz the cucumbers in a processor. Sieve the slush so you get a pale green juice (discard the pulp). Add the lime zest, juice and cordial and churn in an ice-cream maker until frozen. Transfer to a suitable container and freeze. If you don't have an ice-cream maker, freeze the mixture for 1½ hours then remove and scrape into shards with a fork. Return to the freezer and fork up every 30 minutes until it's frozen in icicles.

ELDERFLOWER POSSET

Serves 4-6
- 450ml double cream
- 100g sugar
- Juice of 2 limes
- 3 tbsp elderflower cordial

1 Heat the cream and sugar in a pan over a low heat until the sugar dissolves. Remove and leave to cool a little. Stir in the lime juice and cordial. Pour into little bowls or glasses and chill for at least 2 hours before serving.

PISTACHIO, YOGHURT & ELDERFLOWER CAKE

Serves 8-10
- 250g butter
- 250g sugar
- 150g pistachios, roughly chopped, plus extra, to decorate
- 100g ground almonds
- 200g polenta
- 1 tsp baking powder
- 2 tbsp Greek-style yoghurt
- 3 eggs
- Zest and juice of 1 lemon

Elderflower syrup
- 150ml elderflower cordial
- 2-3 tbsp runny honey
- Lemon juice, to taste

Elderflower icing
- 200g Greek-style yoghurt
- 3 tbsp icing sugar
- 2 tbsp elderflower syrup

1 Preheat the oven to 180C/gas 4. Grease and line the base and sides of a 20cm spring-form cake tin. Beat the butter and sugar until light and fluffy. Add the pistachios, almonds, polenta, baking powder and yoghurt and mix well. Crack in the eggs, one by one, and mix in. Add the lemon zest and juice, stir to combine and pour the mixture into

APRICOT TART

RHUBARB & ORANGE CRUMBLES

APRICOT TART

Serves 8

- 500g puff pastry
- 250g mascarpone
- A few torn basil leaves
- Grated zest of ½ orange
- 8-12 apricots, halved and stoned
- 2 tsp light muscovado sugar

1 Preheat the oven to 200C/gas 6.
Roll out the pastry to a large rectangle,
about 5mm thick, score a 2cm border
and prick inside the border with a fork.
2 Combine the mascarpone, basil leaves
and orange zest in a mixing bowl, then
spread over your pastry. Arrange the
halved apricots, cut-side up, on top.
Dust the tart with the light muscovado
sugar and bake in the oven for 30-40
minutes, until the pastry is golden
and the apricots are tender.

RHUBARB & ORANGE CRUMBLES

Serves 4

- 1kg rhubarb, trimmed, cut into
  5cm pieces
- Finely grated zest and juice of
  1 orange
- 200g soft brown sugar
- 100g cold butter, diced
- 100g flour
- 100g oats

1 Preheat the oven to 180C/gas 4.
Place the rhubarb in a small saucepan
with the orange zest and juice and
1 tablespoon of the sugar. Simmer for
2-3 minutes, till the rhubarb softens.
2 With your fingers, mix the butter into
the flour to make rough crumbs, then
stir in the oats and remaining sugar.
3 Divide the stewed fruit between
4 small ovenproof dishes and top with
the crumble mix. Bake for 25-30 minutes
or till golden. Serve with custard or cream.

BLUEBERRY CAKE

Serves 12

- 225g butter, plus extra for greasing
- 220g caster sugar
- 3 eggs
- 300g self-raising flour
- Grated zest and juice of 1 lemon
- 400g-500g fresh blueberries
- Plain or vanilla yoghurt, to serve

1 Preheat the oven to 175C/gas 3½.
Butter and flour a 25cm spring-form tin.
Line the base with greased greaseproof
paper. Beat the butter and sugar until
creamy, then add the eggs and continue
beating till light and fluffy. Gradually
beat in the flour, lemon zest and juice.
2 Arrange the fruit in a single layer in
the prepared tin then carefully spoon
over the cake batter. Bake in the centre
of the oven for 1-1¼ hours, or until a
skewer inserted into the centre comes
out clean and dry. Remove the cake from
the oven and rest in the tin for 5 minutes
then release and cool on a wire rack
before removing the paper. Best eaten
fresh, with thick yoghurt.

STORE-CUPBOARD FLAPJACKS

Not pictured

**These flapjacks, crammed with fruit
and nuts, are very easy to make.**

Makes 16

- 175g butter
- 6 tbsp honey
- 75g soft light brown sugar
- Finely grated zest of 1 orange
- 75g dried berries
- 50g dried apricots, chopped
- 150g mixed nuts and seeds, chopped
- 300g porridge oats
- 75g wholemeal flour

1 Preheat the oven to 180C/gas 4, and
grease and line a 21cm square cake tin.
2 Melt the butter, honey and sugar in a
saucepan over a medium heat. Add the
remaining ingredients and stir well.
Spoon the mixture into the tin and bake
in the oven for 25-30 minutes, until
golden. Leave to cool in the tin, but slice
into portions while still warm.

EASY
PUDDING

BAKED PEACHES AND RASPBERRIES

BAKED PEACHES & RASPBERRIES

Serves 4

- 4 peaches, halved and stoned
- 1 vanilla pod, split lengthways, seeds scraped
- 50g sugar
- 20g flaked almonds
- 100g raspberries

1 Preheat the oven to 200C/gas 6. Arrange the peaches cut-side up in a roasting tray. Mash the vanilla seeds with 1 teaspoon of sugar then combine with the remaining sugar and scatter half the mixture over the peaches. Bake in the oven for 20 minutes, then scatter over the almonds, berries and remaining sugar. Bake for a further 10 minutes. Serve warm with ice cream or cream.

CARAMEL PEARS

Serves 4

- 4 pears, peeled, halved and cored
- 50g butter
- 75g soft dark brown sugar
- 75ml single cream
- 25g pistachios, chopped

1 Preheat the oven to 200C/gas 6. Arrange the pears in a small baking dish. Melt the butter in a saucepan, add the sugar and stir over a medium heat until dissolved. Pour the caramel over the pears and cover the dish tightly with foil. Bake in the oven for 40 minutes, turning the pears once. When cooked, stir the cream into the caramel, making sure the pears are well coated. Scatter with the pistachios and serve warm.

JAMIE'S PARTY CAKE

Pictured on cover
Serves 24

- 200g unsalted butter, at room temperature
- 600g sugar
- 12 eggs
- 4 tsp good-quality vanilla extract
- 12 tbsp natural red food colouring (optional)
- 8 heaped tbsp cocoa powder
- 600g flour
- 500ml buttermilk
- 2 tsp bicarbonate of soda

CARAMEL PEARS

- 2 tbsp white wine vinegar
- 1-2 punnets each of strawberries, raspberries and blackberries (or a mixture of frozen berries, defrosted)
- Icing sugar, for dusting

Cream cheese frosting

- 300g unsalted butter, at room temperature
- 600g icing sugar
- 450g cream cheese
- 3 tsp vanilla extract
- Grated zest and juice of 2 lemons

1 Preheat the oven to 180C/gas 4 and line the bases of two 25cm cake tins with greaseproof paper.
2 Cream the butter and sugar until light and fluffy. Beat in the eggs, vanilla extract, food colouring, if using, and a pinch of salt. Gradually fold in the cocoa and flour, then stir in the buttermilk.
3 Mix the bicarbonate of soda and white wine vinegar together in a bowl until it fizzes, then stir into the cake batter.

4 Divide the mixture between the lined tins and bake for 25-30 minutes, or until risen and cooked through. Check by inserting a skewer into the centre - if it comes out clean, they're perfect, if not, just pop them back in the oven for another few minutes. Leave to cool in the tin for 15 minutes, then run a knife around the edges and carefully tip onto a wire rack to cool completely.
5 Meanwhile for the cream cheese frosting, cream the butter and icing sugar. Beat the cream cheese in a separate bowl, then add to the butter mixture. Fold in the vanilla extract, lemon zest and juice. Chill until needed.
6 When the cakes are cool, use a spatula to spread a layer of frosting over 1 cake then add some of your mixed berries - as many as you like. Carefully place the other cake on top and spread the rest of the frosting over the surface. Top with the remaining berries, then use a sieve to dust over a little icing sugar to finish.

RHUBARB CORDIAL

Cordial relations

Cordial is also delicious in mixed drinks. Add 1 part cordial to 1-2 parts scotch and a dash of ginger syrup, then lengthen with soda. For a special occasion, pour a little cordial in champagne flutes, add a splash of Grand Marnier, then top up with cava or prosecco. Or add to a glass with a shot of vodka, and top up with blood orange juice and soda. To make a cordial with seasonal fruit, follow the basic method, adjusting the sugar as necessary - sweeter fruits will need less. When making plum cordial, add a stick of cinnamon and some chopped ginger, so you have a spicy blend that's nice in cooler months. For an easy berry cordial, squash 500g each of fruit and sugar to a mush in a bowl, then add 250ml boiling water and leave to cool. Strain through a cloth and store in sterilised bottles.

HIGHLAND MORNING
Serves 2
- 90ml whisky
- 30ml Cointreau
- Juice of ½ grapefruit
- Twists of grapefruit rind, to garnish

1 Shake the whisky, Cointreau, juice and lots of crushed ice in a cocktail shaker. Strain into chilled glasses, then garnish with twists of grapefruit rind.

SANTO MANHATTAN
Recipe from Fifteen London
Serves 1
- Peeled zest of 1 orange
- 50ml rye whisky
- 35ml vin santo (Italian dessert wine)

1 Place most of the orange zest in a cocktail shaker and bash with a wooden spoon to release the flavour. Fill the shaker with ice and pour over the whisky and vin santo. Stir for 1 minute then strain into a chilled martini glass. Garnish with more orange zest.

RHUBARB CORDIAL
Makes 1 litre
- 1.5kg rhubarb, roughly chopped
- At least 750g caster sugar
- At least 75ml lemon juice

1 Place the rhubarb and 75ml water in a pan over a low heat and cook till the rhubarb starts releasing its juices. Turn the heat up a little and continue cooking until the rhubarb is completely soft.
2 Line a mixing bowl with clean muslin and tip in the rhubarb. Tie the corners of the muslin together. Suspend the bag over the bowl for several hours to drain.
3 For every litre of juice add 750g sugar and 75ml lemon juice. Stir in a pan over a medium heat to dissolve the sugar - don't let it boil. Serve diluted with water.

IRISH COFFEE
Serves 1
- 50ml Irish whiskey
- 1 tsp soft light brown sugar
- 150ml hot, strong, black coffee
- 1-2 tbsp double cream

1 Pour the whiskey into a mug and stir in the sugar. Stir in the coffee so the sugar dissolves. Pour the cream over the back of a spoon that's just touching the surface of the coffee, so it floats on top.

SUMMER REFRESHER
Makes about 1 litre
- Flesh of 1 pineapple
- 2 grapefruits, peeled
- 4 apples
- ¼-½ bunch of mint

1 Chop the ingredients to a manageable size, then press through a juicer for a fresh and zesty summer juice.

RHUBARB CORDIAL

Cordial relations

Cordial is also delicious in mixed drinks. Add 1 part cordial to 1-2 parts scotch and a dash of ginger syrup, then lengthen with soda. For a special occasion, pour a little cordial in champagne flutes, add a splash of Grand Marnier, then top up with cava or prosecco. Or add to a glass with a shot of vodka, and top up with blood orange juice and soda. To make a cordial with seasonal fruit, follow the basic method, adjusting the sugar as necessary - sweeter fruits will need less. When making plum cordial, add a stick of cinnamon and some chopped ginger, so you have a spicy blend that's nice in cooler months. For an easy berry cordial, squash 500g each of fruit and sugar to a mush in a bowl, then add 250ml boiling water and leave to cool. Strain through a cloth and store in sterilised bottles.

HIGHLAND MORNING
Serves 2
- 90ml whisky
- 30ml Cointreau
- Juice of ½ grapefruit
- Twists of grapefruit rind, to garnish

1 Shake the whisky, Cointreau, juice and lots of crushed ice in a cocktail shaker. Strain into chilled glasses, then garnish with twists of grapefruit rind.

SANTO MANHATTAN
Recipe from Fifteen London
Serves 1
- Peeled zest of 1 orange
- 50ml rye whisky
- 35ml vin santo (Italian dessert wine)

1 Place most of the orange zest in a cocktail shaker and bash with a wooden spoon to release the flavour. Fill the shaker with ice and pour over the whisky and vin santo. Stir for 1 minute then strain into a chilled martini glass. Garnish with more orange zest.

RHUBARB CORDIAL
Makes 1 litre
- 1.5kg rhubarb, roughly chopped
- At least 750g caster sugar
- At least 75ml lemon juice

1 Place the rhubarb and 75ml water in a pan over a low heat and cook till the rhubarb starts releasing its juices. Turn the heat up a little and continue cooking until the rhubarb is completely soft.
2 Line a mixing bowl with clean muslin and tip in the rhubarb. Tie the corners of the muslin together. Suspend the bag over the bowl for several hours to drain.
3 For every litre of juice add 750g sugar and 75ml lemon juice. Stir in a pan over a medium heat to dissolve the sugar - don't let it boil. Serve diluted with water.

IRISH COFFEE
Serves 1
- 50ml Irish whiskey
- 1 tsp soft light brown sugar
- 150ml hot, strong, black coffee
- 1-2 tbsp double cream

1 Pour the whiskey into a mug and stir in the sugar. Stir in the coffee so the sugar dissolves. Pour the cream over the back of a spoon that's just touching the surface of the coffee, so it floats on top.

SUMMER REFRESHER
Makes about 1 litre
- Flesh of 1 pineapple
- 2 grapefruits, peeled
- 4 apples
- ¼-½ bunch of mint

1 Chop the ingredients to a manageable size, then press through a juicer for a fresh and zesty summer juice.

BISHOP

WINTER BOOST JUICE

BISHOP

Recipe by Nick Strangeway

This is a mulled-wine punch, perfect served warm or chilled at Christmas.

Serves about 8

- 3 lemons
- 4 oranges
- 60 cloves
- 250ml water
- 3 allspice berries
- 1 cinnamon stick
- 2cm ginger, grated
- ⅛ whole nutmeg, grated
- 700ml full-bodied red wine, such as cabernet sauvignon
- 125ml pedro ximénez sherry
- 150g sugar
- Zest of 1 small lemon, juice of ½
- Orange slices and grated nutmeg, to serve

1 Preheat the oven to 180C/gas 4. Stud each lemon and orange with 8 cloves and bake in the oven for 15 minutes, until the fruit is starting to caramelise. When done, remove the cloves.
2 Meanwhile, place the remaining cloves in a pan over a low heat with the water and spices. Pour in the wine and sherry. As it starts to simmer, add the sugar and lemon zest and juice. Simmer for 5-10 minutes then add the citrus, crushing to release the oils and juice. Strain through muslin and serve or transfer to sterilised bottles, to chill for later use. To serve, heat and garnish with orange slices and grated nutmeg.

HOT CHOCOLATE

Serves 4

- 700ml milk
- 100g dark chocolate, bashed up
- Whipped cream and grated chocolate

1 Heat the milk in a pan. Just before it boils, take it off the heat and whisk in the chocolate until smooth. Serve topped with cream and extra chocolate.

WINTER BOOST JUICE

Makes about 1 litre

- 6 carrots, trimmed
- 4 oranges, peeled and halved
- 4 apples, quartered
- 2.5cm piece of fresh ginger

1 Press the ingredients through a juicer for a reviving juice.

LEMON ICED TEA

Serves 4-6

- 2 earl grey tea bags
- 1 litre just-boiled water
- 100ml sugar syrup
- 4 lemons - 2 juiced, 2 finely sliced

1 Place the tea bags in a large jug and pour over the just-boiled water. Leave to steep for 10 minutes, then add the sugar syrup and lemon juice and slices. Refrigerate until ready to serve, then top up the jug with ice cubes.

ZURRA

White wine sangria

Serves 4

- 50g sugar
- 2 cinnamon sticks
- 150ml water
- A handful of mint leaves
- 1 lemon, sliced
- 1 orange, sliced
- 1 peach, sliced
- 6 strawberries, sliced
- 375 white wine
- Soda water or lemonade
- Ice cubes, to serve

1 Put the sugar, cinnamon, water and half the mint in a pan. Bring to the boil then simmer for 5 minutes. Allow to cool.
2 Place the fruit in a large jug. Add the sugar syrup and white wine and stir. Top up with soda water or lemonade. Add the remaining mint leaves and a few ice cubes, if you wish.
3 To serve, place ice cubes in glasses and fill with sangria, making sure that some fruit is added to each glass.

FENNEL ICED TEA

CITRON PRESSE

FENNEL ICED TEA
Serves 2
- 1 fennel bulb, sliced
- 1 lapsang souchong tea bag
- 2 tsp honey
- ½ lemon, sliced

1 Infuse the fennel and tea bag in 600ml of just-boiled water for 5 minutes; discard the tea bag. Cool. Stir in honey, add lemon, pour over ice and serve.

CITRON PRESSE
- Lemons, juiced
- 1 tsp caster sugar for each lemon used

1 Put lemon juice and sugar in a jug. Stir till the sugar dissolves. Place some ice cubes or crushed ice in glasses and pour over the lemon and sugar mixture. Add water to taste, stir and serve.

LEMON VERBENA TEA
Serves 2
- 4 lemon verbena sprigs, leaves picked (or 2–3 tbsp dried leaves)
- ½ lemon, sliced
- 500ml just-boiled water
- Honey, to taste (optional)

1 Steep the lemon verbena leaves and all but 2 of the lemon slices in the just-boiled water for about 5 minutes. Strain into tea cups. Add a slice of lemon to each cup to serve, and sweeten with honey, if you like.

GINGER, LEMON & MINT SLUSHIE
Serves 4
- 40g fresh ginger, chopped
- Juice of ½ lemon
- 10g mint leaves, plus extra to garnish
- 150g sugar
- 1 litre water
- Vodka (optional)

1 Place the ginger, lemon juice, mint, sugar and water in a pan. Slowly bring to the boil, allowing the sugar to dissolve, then simmer for 5 minutes. Leave to cool. Strain into an ice-cream machine and churn for 20 minutes, or until it reaches the consistency of a slushie. Pour into glasses and add a shot of vodka, if you like. Garnish with mint.

COMPLETE BREAKFAST SMOOTHIE
Serves 4
- 50g oats
- 50g wheatgerm
- 200ml milk
- 1 tbsp honey
- 5 tbsp plain yoghurt, plus 2 tbsp extra (optional)
- 200g raspberries
- 200g blueberries
- ½ tsp vanilla extract (optional)
- 10 ice cubes

1 Blitz the oats and wheatgerm in a blender or food processor. Add the milk, honey and yoghurt, and blitz to combine. Add the berries, plus extra yoghurt and vanilla extract, if you like. Add the ice cubes and pulse till combined.

SEASONAL SMOOTHIE
Agave syrup or nectar comes from a Mexican plant and is used as a sweetener. You can find it in selected supermarkets. It's often used as a vegan alternative to honey, which you can use here instead, if you prefer.
Serves 2–3
- 100g blueberries
- 100g raspberries
- 150g strawberries
- 200ml orange juice
- 250g plain yoghurt
- 2 tbsp agave syrup
- A few basil leaves

1 Blitz the fruit, orange juice, yoghurt and syrup in a food processor, then serve topped with basil leaves.

GINGER & MINT TEA

GINGER & MINT TEA
Serves 2-4
- A thumb-sized piece of ginger, sliced
- ½ bunch of mint

1 Steep the ginger and the mint in boiled water for 3-5 minutes. Strain, then serve garnished with mint leaves.

HOT TODDY
Serves 2
- 100ml whisky, or more if you're feeling festive
- 250ml freshly boiled water
- 4 tbsp honey
- 2 lemon slices
- 2 cinnamon sticks
- 2 whole cloves

1 Heat all the ingredients together in a saucepan for 3-4 minutes. Serve hot.

SUPERNOVA ELDERFLOWER CHAMPAGNE
The natural yeast in elderflowers adds fizz to this drink. The amount of yeast in the flowers depends on when in the season they are picked, and whether the sun has been shining. You can add a pinch of dried yeast if your flowers are a little lacklustre. Sturdy glass bottles with a hinge top, or thick plastic screw-top bottles are a must to prevent corks popping early. You also need a clean 8-litre bucket or basin, plus a large piece of muslin or a clean thin tea towel.
Makes about 8 litres
- 30 elderflower heads
- Grated zest and juice of 6 lemons
- 1.1kg sugar
- 2 tbsp white wine vinegar
- A pinch of dried yeast (optional)

1 Gently shake the elderflower heads to get rid of any bits or bugs. Place the lemon zest and juice in the bucket with the sugar and vinegar. Add 4 litres of hot water, stir the sugar to dissolve, then add 4 litres of cold water. Cover with muslin or a cloth and leave in a warm place for 24 hours to ferment.
2 After 24 hours, check if fermentation has started. If it has, there will be some bubbles on the surface. If there aren't any bubbles, add a tiny pinch of yeast. Leave the mixture, covered with muslin, for another 48 hours.
3 Strain through the muslin into a clean jug, then pour into sterilised bottles and seal tightly. Leave in a cool place for at least 2 weeks. It'll be best if you can wait as long as a month, after which it can be chilled. Your elderflower bubbles should keep like this for up to a year.

MARATHON SMOOTHIE
The best smoothie by 26.2 miles!
Makes about 1.25 litres
- 1 ripe avocado, peeled and stoned
- 1 large cucumber, peeled
- 2 kiwi fruit, peeled
- 500ml apple juice
- 10-12 ice cubes

1 Blitz it all up in a blender till smooth!

COLD COMFORT
Serves 2
- Juice of 1 each lemon and orange
- 2 pieces of stem ginger, chopped, and 2-3 tsp of the syrup
- 30ml whisky (optional)

1 Place all the ingredients in a large mug, then top up with boiling water. Allow to steep, and strain the ginger pieces, if you like.

RASPBERRY SPAGLIATO

Prosecco, please

The options are endless when it comes to prosecco, as its refreshing citrus tones complement almost everything. In winter, pour it into pomegranate juice, adding a few pomegranate seeds, too. It's great with blood orange; add a drop or two of Angostura bitters for an extra flavour twist. For a mojito-style drink, combine prosecco with a little lime juice and some bashed-up mint. For a bitter-sweet drink, mix prosecco with grapefruit juice and a dash of Campari. Of course, you can make a classic apéritif by topping up a measure of Aperol with prosecco. In the summer, mash up raspberries, douse them in Cointreau and top up with fizz. If you don't have any fresh fruit, have a look in your cupboard as fruit in syrup (such as lychees) is great; make sure you get some in each glass.

RASPBERRY SPAGLIATO

Recipe by Nick Strangeway

Don't break out the champagne for this sparkling cocktail that's perfect at Christmas. It may be a cheaper option, but prosecco's fruitiness really works well with the drink, and cava would be another, good-value choice.

Serves 2
- 10 frozen raspberries
- 2 tsp sugar
- 25ml Campari
- 25ml Lillet Rouge, or any sweet vermouth
- 125ml prosecco

1 Muddle the raspberries with the sugar in a cocktail shaker. Add the Campari and Lillet Rouge and give the drink a gentle shake, then strain into an ice-filled glass and top with prosecco.

LEMONGRASS & GRAPEFRUIT VODKA

A bottle of flavoured spirits makes an impressive gift for the minimal effort that's required. You could also add a bit of ginger to this.

Makes 750ml
- 3 lemongrass stalks, outer layers discarded, roughly chopped
- 750ml vodka
- 1 small pink grapefruit

1 Put the lemongrass in a large, clean, airtight jar with the vodka. Shake and leave it somewhere dark for 24 hours.
2 Pierce the grapefruit all over with a skewer. Pop it in the jar and shake it up again. Return the jar to the dark place, shaking it a couple of times a day. After another 2 days, have a taste to check the flavours. If you want them stronger, leave it for a few days longer and taste again. Strain through some fine muslin and transfer to a sterilised bottle.

THE BRAMBLE

Recipe From Bramble, Edinburgh

Created by Dick Bradsell at Fred's Club, London, in the 1980s this drink inspired the naming of one of Edinburgh's most decorated bars. A perfect tipple for the summer sun, or equally the Edinburgh drizzle.

Serves 1
- 2 shots of gin
- 25ml fresh lemon juice
- 2 tsp sugar syrup (a mix of 2 parts sugar to 1 part water)
- Crème de mure (blackberry liqueur)
- Lemon slice and blackberries, to garnish

1 Pour gin, lemon juice and syrup into a shaker with ice. Shake and pour over crushed ice in an old-fashioned glass. Pour crème de mure over the top to create a bleeding effect and garnish with the lemon and blackberries.

HOT BUTTERED RUM

POMEGRANATE SOUR

HOT BUTTERED RUM

Makes enough to last all winter!
- 250g butter
- 250g brown sugar
- 250g icing sugar
- 500ml vanilla ice cream, softened
- 1½ tsp ground cinnamon, plus a pinch
- 1½ tsp ground nutmeg, plus a pinch
- Spiced rum

1 Melt the butter in a saucepan over a low heat. Mix in both sugars and stir until dissolved. Remove from the heat and mix in the softened ice cream and the spices. Place in a suitable freezer-proof container and place in the freezer.
2 To serve, place 35–50ml spiced rum in each person's mug and top with 2 tablespoons of ice-cream mix. Fill the mugs with just-boiled water and scatter over a pinch of cinnamon or nutmeg.

POMEGRANATE SOUR

Serves 1
- 1 shot vodka
- 3 shots pomegranate syrup (see page 160)
- Juice of 1 lemon
- Soda water, to top up

1 In a cocktail shaker, shake up the vodka, syrup and lemon juice. Pour into a glass, over ice. Top up with soda water.

CHRISTMAS VODKA

You'll need a bigger bottle for this festive spirit, to fit all the cranberries.
Makes 750ml
- 250g cranberries, fresh or frozen
- 750ml vodka
- 100g sugar
- 5 cloves, 1 nutmeg, cracked, 1 vanilla pod, 1 tsp allspice berries (optional)

1 Prick the cranberries and pop into a sterilised bottle with the vodka and sugar. Then add the spices, if you like.
2 Place in the freezer and shake regularly until the flavours are infused and the vodka is a pretty pink. Serve on the rocks or with soda.

NEW YORK-STYLE EGG CREAM

Serves 2
- 100ml cold whole milk
- 300–400ml cold soda water
- 2 tbsp chocolate syrup

1 Divide the milk between 2 glasses. Top up with soda water, pouring it against the side of the glass, leaving 2–3cm of room at the top. Pour in the chocolate syrup and use a teaspoon to stir until the syrup dissolves and you have a chocolate-coloured drink with a creamy-white, foamy top.

MULLED WINE

Having a few spice sachets stored in an airtight container means giving a homemade present is easy – just attach one to a bottle of wine (but remember to keep a few for yourself).
Makes 750ml
- 750ml red wine
- ½ orange, sliced
- 2–3 tbsp sugar

Spice sachet
- 8cm cinnamon stick
- 1 tsp cloves
- 20 allspice berries
- 3 cardamom pods
- 1 tsp chopped candied orange peel

1 For the spice sachet, snap the cinnamon in half and place in a muslin square (or tea-bag case) with the remaining ingredients. Tie with string.
2 Place the sachet in a pan with the red wine, orange and sugar. Bring to the boil. Reduce the heat and simmer for 15 minutes. Serve hot.

CHOCOLATE SWIZZLES
- Cinnamon sticks
- Dark chocolate (70% cocoa), melted

1 Dip the cinnamon sticks in the melted chocolate, then put aside to set. Use the sticks to stir coffee, hot milk or cocoa.

Bake something delicious to make a difference

Get together with your friends, family or colleagues and throw a fabulous baking party! Then spend an afternoon catching up and enjoying gorgeous home-made cakes, while raising money for people with a learning disability.

Find out more: email **bakewithme@mencap.org.uk** call **020 7696 6983** or visit **www.bakewithme.org.uk**

The voice of learning disability

Charity number 222377 (England, Northern Ireland and Wales); SCO41079 (Scotland)   2010.185–07.11

SAUCES & EXTRAS

BASIL OIL

Infused oils

Flavoured oils are an easy way to jazz up a meal. Woody herbs such as rosemary work well. Just put a few sprigs in a sterilised bottle and top with olive oil. Swap the basil in the recipe below for marjoram and you'll have an ideal oil for summer salads. Or try thyme paired with lemon peel. You could roast a few garlic cloves and drop them in olive oil – it's delicious on pizza – or make a classic chilli oil by combining varieties of dried chillies in olive oil; smoky chipotle would be especially good. Be adventurous and experiment with leftover parmesan rinds in olive oil, or even some bashed up anchovies. For Asian-inspired oils, bash a lemongrass stem and a few kaffir lime leaves and add to peanut oil, or fry sliced ginger in peanut oil until brown, strain, and use as a base for Asian-style dressings.

BASIL OIL
Makes 400ml
- 400ml olive oil
- 25g basil, leaves only

1 Place the oil and basil in a mini food processor and blitz until combined. Transfer to a saucepan and simmer for 5 minutes. Remove from the heat, cool for 30 minutes then strain through a funnel lined with muslin or paper towel into a sterilised bottle. Use to finish pasta dishes, tomato salads or risottos.

CRANBERRY SAUCE
For your Christmas ham or turkey.
Makes 750g
- 500g cranberries (defrosted if frozen)
- 200g soft brown sugar
- 1 cinnamon stick
- 5 cloves
- Peeled zest and juice of 1 orange
- 180ml port

1 Place all ingredients in a large pan and simmer, stirring occasionally, for 15–20 minutes until thickened. Taste the sauce; if it's too sour, add a little more sugar. Allow to cool slightly before removing the cinnamon stick and peel. Try to find all the cloves and remove them too; your guests won't appreciate crunching down on stray ones. Serve warm or at room temperature.

BRANDY BUTTER
- 100g unsalted butter, at room temperature
- 100g icing sugar, sieved
- 2 tbsp brandy (or more, if you like)
- A splash of hot water

1 Cream together the butter and icing sugar until smooth and pale, then beat in the brandy and hot water. Chill to firm up, then when ready, serve with Christmas pudding and mince pies.

SAGE & CHESTNUT STUFFING
You can, of course, cook this in the neck cavity of a turkey.
Serves 14 with turkey
- 750g sausage meat
- 2 apples, grated
- 2 onions, grated
- A large handful of breadcrumbs
- 250g vacuum-packed chestnuts
- ½ bunch of sage, leaves picked
- 1 egg
- Olive oil

1 Preheat the oven to 200C/gas 6. Put the meat in a large bowl. Add the apples, onions and breadcrumbs. Crumble in the chestnuts and snip in the sage (reserve 4 leaves). Season, then crack in the egg and scrunch with your hands.
2 Place the stuffing in a 30cm x 16cm ovenproof dish and scatter over the reserved sage. Drizzle with olive oil and bake for 45 minutes until golden.

NUTTY STUFFED DATES; PEPPERMINT CREAMS

INSTANT PICKLED ONIONS

NUTTY STUFFED DATES

Makes 18
- 150g golden marzipan
- 18 medjool dates
- 18 walnut halves

1 Roll the marzipan into a sausage and cut into 18 pieces. Stuff each date with a piece of the marzipan and then push a walnut half into each one.

PEPPERMINT CREAMS

Children will love making this recipe.
Makes 22-25
- 1 egg white
- A squeeze of lemon juice
- 400g icing sugar, plus extra for dusting
- ½ tsp peppermint extract

1 Lightly beat the egg white in a bowl. When it starts to foam, squeeze in a drop of lemon juice. Sift in the icing sugar and peppermint and combine. When it gets too tough with a spoon, bring together with your hands. Transfer to a surface dusted with icing sugar. Dust the mixture with icing sugar, then roll to 2cm thick. Cut into circles with a pastry cutter (approx 3.5cm across) and transfer to a tray dusted in icing sugar to dry out.

INSTANT PICKLED ONIONS

This is a cheat's version as you can eat them right away, although it's worth waiting a week or two for the flavours to develop. Great on a ploughman's platter or a British-cheese sarnie.
Makes two 1-litre jars
- 500ml red wine vinegar
- ½ bunch of thyme
- 500ml white wine vinegar
- 4 bay leaves
- 500g red onions
- 500g white onions

1 Get 2 pans and add 1 tablespoon of salt to each. Add the red wine vinegar and thyme to one pan and the white wine vinegar and bay to the other.
2 Keeping the colours separate, slice the onions using your food processor, or do them finely with a knife.
3 Place both pans over a high heat and bring to the boil. Place the red onions in the pan with red wine vinegar and the white onions in the other pan. Reduce the heat to medium and cook for 2-3 minutes, pushing the onions down with the back of a wooden spoon to stop them rising to the surface.
4 As soon as the onions have softened, use a slotted spoon to transfer them into sterilised jars. Ladle over the vinegar, then close the lids and leave to cool. These can be eaten straight away, but if you leave them for at least 2 weeks they'll taste amazing.

BLACKBERRY, HAZELNUT & APPLE SAUCE

On colder nights, you could also cook this sauce over a low heat.
Serves 2
- 150g blackberries
- 30g hazelnuts, toasted
- 1 apple, peeled and cored
- Juice of ½ lemon
- 1 tsp sugar
- A pinch of cinnamon

1 Place all the ingredients in a mini food processor and blitz until roughly chopped. Serve over vanilla ice cream.

VANILLA SUGAR

- 1-2 vanilla pods, split lengthways
- Golden caster sugar

1 A perfect gift for those on a budget to make, this will be appreciated by keen bakers. Add the vanilla to an airtight jar (choose a pretty one) and fill with the sugar. Tie a ribbon round the jar, and attach a baking recipe and a note to shake the jar occasionally.

PICCALILLI

with plastic or rubber seals. Keep in a cool, dark place for up to 6 months. Refrigerate the jars once open and use within 4 weeks.

HARICOT, PAPRIKA & FENNEL HUMMUS
Serves 4
- 1 x 400g tin haricot beans, drained
- ½ tsp smoked paprika
- 2 tsp fennel seeds
- 3 tbsp tahini
- 3 tbsp olive oil
- Juice of 1 lemon
- Pita crisps, to serve

1 Place all the ingredients in a mini food processor and blitz until smooth. Season with sea salt and freshly ground black pepper. Serve with pita crisps.

POMEGRANATE SYRUP
Makes about 400ml
- 500ml pomegranate juice
- 200ml caster sugar

1 Place the juice and sugar in a pan and bring to the boil, stirring occasionally. Once the sugar has dissolved, reduce the heat and simmer, skimming any foam, for 8–10 minutes, or until reduced by half. Remove from the heat and allow to cool. Transfer to a sterilised jar and store in the fridge for up to 2 weeks.

SICHUAN RUB
Serves 4
- 2 tbsp sichuan peppercorns
- 2 garlic cloves, grated
- A thumb-sized knob of ginger, grated
- Grated zest of 2 limes
- Sesame oil

1 Bash the peppercorns using a pestle and mortar until ground. Season, add the garlic, ginger and lime zest and bash the rub together a bit more.
2 This is a delicious for grilled fish. Slash the skin, rub in the mix, drizzle with sesame oil then grill or roast till cooked. It will also go well on pork chops.

PICCALILLI
Makes about 1kg
- 650ml malt vinegar
- 2 tbsp coriander seeds, lightly crushed
- 1 carrot, chopped into 1cm pieces
- 3 large shallots, sliced
- 1 head of cauliflower, broken up into small florets
- 3 tbsp flour
- 3 tbsp mustard powder
- 1 tsp ground ginger
- 1 tbsp turmeric
- 100ml cider vinegar
- 3 baby courgettes, halved lengthways and sliced (or 1 small–medium courgette, quartered and sliced)
- 80g green beans, chopped
- 3 garlic cloves, sliced
- 220g sugar

1 Place the malt vinegar in a large pan with the crushed coriander seeds and bring to the boil. Stir in the carrot, shallots and cauliflower, reduce the heat and simmer for 4–5 minutes. The vegetables should still be quite crunchy.
2 Meanwhile, mix together the flour, mustard powder, ginger and turmeric then slowly add the cider vinegar, whisking continuously until you have a smooth paste. Set aside.
3 Add the courgettes, beans, garlic and sugar to the pan of vegetables and cook, stirring occasionally, for 2–3 minutes, or until the sugar has dissolved. Drain the vegetables in a colander over a large bowl, reserving the drained vinegar.
4 Put the mustard mixture in the empty pan over a medium heat. Gradually whisk in the drained vinegar and bring to a simmer. Continue cooking, stirring frequently, for 10–12 minutes, until the mixture has thickened (it should be a little bit like a loose custard).
5 Return the drained vegetables to the pan and gently stir through the sauce until everything is coated. Remove from the heat and transfer to sterilised jars

APRICOT & VANILLA JAM

Makes enough for three 350ml jars

- 1kg apricots, halved and stoned
- 700g granulated sugar
- 2 vanilla pods, split

1 Place the fruit in a large pan with the sugar, vanilla pods and 200ml water. Slowly bring up to the boil, allowing the sugar to dissolve, and then simmer for 1 hour. Store in sterilised jars, then serve with toast or scones.

PEANUT BUTTER

Makes 220g

- 200g peanuts
- 2 tbsp groundnut oil
- A pinch of sugar
- A pinch of salt

1 Blitz all ingredients, except 50g peanuts, in a food processor until completely smooth. Add remaining peanuts and pulse until roughly chopped. Serve on hot toast.

GOOSEBERRY & ELDERFLOWER JAM

Makes enough for six 340ml jars

- 2kg gooseberries
- 12 elderflower heads, or 100ml elderflower cordial
- 750g sugar
- 2 vanilla pods, split lengthways and seeds scraped

1 Top and tail the gooseberries, discarding the hard ends, and place in a large saucepan. If you're using elderflowers, tie them up in a piece of muslin and secure with string, then add to the saucepan. If using cordial, add to the pan with 150ml water. Bring to the boil, then reduce the heat and simmer for about 30 minutes, or until the fruit is tender and has broken down. Remove from the heat, squeeze any liquid out of the elderflower parcel and discard.
2 Add the sugar and the vanilla pod and seeds to the pan and boil over a high heat for about 10 minutes, skimming off any foam that forms on the surface.

APRICOT & VANILLA JAM

Pour through a strainer into sterilised jars and leave to cool before putting sealing with the lids.

CHAR-GRILLED RED PEPPER SAUCE

- 2 red peppers, halved
- 1 tomato
- ½ red chilli
- 100g ground almonds
- 4 tbsp extra-virgin olive oil

1 Grill the peppers until the skin is blackened, then put in a bowl and cover with clingfilm. Leave them to steam for 30 minutes, then remove the skin and seeds.
2 Chop and deseed the tomato and the red chilli, then whizz in a blender with the peppers, almonds and oil until smooth. Season with sea salt and freshly ground pepper. Serve with chorizo and rocket in a sandwich.

VEGETARIAN GRAVY

Serves 6

- 1 red onion, skin on, cut into wedges
- 1 white onion, skin on, cut into wedges
- 1 celery stalk, cut into 1cm chunks
- 2 carrots, cut into 1cm chunks
- 1 red pepper, cut into 3cm wedges
- 2 tomatoes, cut into 3cm wedges
- Sprigs of rosemary, sage and bay
- Olive oil
- 3 tbsp soy sauce
- 2 tbsp plain flour
- 600ml vegetable stock, simmering

1 Preheat oven to 180C/gas 4. Put the veg and herbs in a roasting tray. Drizzle with olive oil and soy. Season and toss. Roast for 30 minutes, till cooked through.
2 Transfer the tray to a medium-heat hob. Add a drizzle of oil and the flour to the veg and cook for 3 minutes, stirring. Add the stock. Mash the veg. Bring to a boil. Simmer until thickened. Sieve into a pan. Heat, season and serve.

SALSA VERDE FRESCO
SALSA ROJA

- 1 cinnamon stick
- 6 cloves
- 150ml cider vinegar

1 Cook the tomatoes in a saucepan of simmering water for 5 minutes. Drain, cool slightly, remove the stem ends and purée in a blender.
2 Heat the oil in a large frying pan over a medium heat until shimmering. Add the chillies, onion, garlic, cinnamon, cloves and a pinch of salt and cook, stirring, until the onion has softened.
3 Add the tomatoes and vinegar and simmer, stirring often, until thickened and slightly sweet – about 15 minutes. Taste for salt, then put the whole lot in the blender and whizz until smooth.
4 Pour into sterilised bottles, where your punchy sauce will keep for a few weeks in the fridge.

GREEN OLIVE TAPENADE

Serves 2
- 100g green olives, stoned
- ½ red onion, cut into wedges
- 1 tbsp pine nuts, toasted
- 2 tbsp chopped parsley
- 2 tbsp olive oil

1 Place all ingredients in a processor and blitz to roughly chop. Season with pepper and stir through pasta.

EASY HARISSA

- 2 large red chillies, deseeded, chopped
- 2 garlic cloves, chopped
- 1 tsp caraway seeds
- 1 tsp ground cumin
- 1 tsp ground coriander
- 1 tsp paprika
- 3 piquillo peppers (see note)
- ¼ tsp salt
- Olive oil

1 In a food processor, blitz all the ingredients with enough olive oil to make a paste. Serve drizzled over grilled red mullet or chicken. Store any leftover harissa in the fridge.
Note Piquillo peppers are mild chilli peppers, roasted and sold in jars.

SALSA VERDE FRESCO

This is insanely fresh, yet deep and smoky at the same time. Eat it rough and ready, or blend to a velvety sauce.
Makes 750g (800ml)
- 2 large green chillies, ideally serrano
- 12 green tomatillos or green tomatoes, skinned and halved
- 2 onions, cut into wedges
- 1 garlic clove, roughly chopped
- A small bunch of coriander, leaves picked
- 1 avocado, quartered
- Juice of 2 limes

1 Heat a griddle pan until very hot. Char-grill the chillies until their skins are black and blistered. Place in a bowl, cover with clingfilm and set aside.
2 In batches, char-grill the tomatillos or green tomatoes and onions until they're blackened and caramelised on all sides.
3 Meanwhile, remove the chillies from the bowl and peel off the blackened skin. If you prefer a milder flavour, take out the seeds. Now, decide whether you want to go chunky or smooth...
4 For a textured, chopped salsa, place the chillies, tomatillos, onions, garlic, coriander leaves and avocado on a big board. Chop everything, melding all the flavours together, until the ingredients are all about the same size. Mix in the lime juice, and season.
5 For a smooth, bottled salsa, blitz all the ingredients in a blender. Pour into sterilised bottles and keep in the fridge for up to a week.

SALSA ROJA

Makes 525g (600ml)
- 12 ripe plum tomatoes
- 3 tbsp olive oil
- 6-8 dried chillies (the long, thin arbol variety are best), whole
- 1 onion, sliced
- 1 garlic clove, sliced

ROCKET PESTO

CHOCOLATE TRUFFLES

ROCKET PESTO

Serves 6 (in pasta)

- 150g rocket
- 50g parmesan, grated
- 2 tbsp blanched hazelnuts
- 4 tbsp extra-virgin olive oil
- ¼ tsp salt
- Grated zest and juice of ½ lemon

1 Blitz the rocket, parmesan and nuts in a food processor until roughly chopped. Add the remaining ingredients and blitz again until combined. Season and store in a sterilised jar. Serve on toast, or stir through pasta or risotto.

CHOCOLATE TRUFFLES

Makes 50-60

- 275ml double cream
- 50g unsalted butter
- 300g dark (70% cocoa) chocolate, broken into small pieces
- A splash of any alcohol, such as brandy, Cointreau, chocolate liqueur or rum (optional)
- Cocoa powder, to dust, or finely sliced pistachios or praline, to coat (see note)

1 Heat the double cream in a saucepan over a low heat, then stir in the butter to combine. Put the broken chocolate in a bowl and pour the hot cream over it, stirring until the chocolate has melted.

Add a pinch of sea salt and a splash of your chosen alcohol, if desired. Once it's all smooth and silky, pour into a bowl and leave to set.
2 Use a teaspoon to shape the mixture into small irregular truffles and place on a tray lined with greaseproof paper. To finish, dip the chocolates in cocoa, finely sliced pistachio nuts or praline.
Note To make the praline, toast 50g hazelnuts in a dry pan, then set aside. Put 100g sugar in the pan with 2 tablespoons water and gently heat without stirring until you have a golden caramel. Throw the nuts back in and coat with caramel, then pour onto an oiled tray and allow to set. Once hard, break up and blitz in the food processor

APRICOT CURD

Makes about 1 litre

- 700g apricots, halved, stones removed
- 220g sugar
- 4 eggs
- 125g butter, diced
- 20-30ml lemon juice
- Meringues, to serve

1 Cook the apricots in a saucepan with enough water to just cover them until they are soft. Pour off half the cooking liquid. Transfer the fruit and remaining juices to a food processor, add the sugar

and purée until smooth. Cool a little, then strain and chill until cold.
2 Beat the eggs with an electric whisk until creamy, then fold through the purée. Transfer to a saucepan and cook over a low heat, stirring. Gradually add the butter as the mixture thickens. Add lemon juice to taste. Cool, stirring occasionally. Store covered in the fridge until required. Serve with meringues or use to flavour ice cream or custard, or as a filling for pastries.

SPICED CLEMENTINE SAUCE

Full of spicy, Christmassy flavours.

Makes 350ml

- 150g sugar
- 1 vanilla pod, split
- 5 cloves
- 1 cinnamon stick
- Juice of 6-8 clementines

1 In a saucepan, gently heat the sugar, vanilla pod, cloves and cinnamon with 100ml water until the sugar dissolves. Remove from the heat and add the clementine juice. Leave to infuse for 15 minutes then strain and pour into a sterilised bottle, or a jug if using immediately. Keeps, chilled, for 2 days. Delicious with fruit salads, ice cream or steamed sponge pudding.

Yearbook index